BORN AGAIN CHRIST'S VERSION

Understanding the Biblical Born-Again Experience

JUN P. ESPINA

Happyprime Corporation

BORN AGAIN CHRIST'S VERSION: Understanding the Biblical Born-Again Experience

ISBN: 978-621-8236-06-6

Published by Happyprime Corporation
Ruby Subdivision, Catalunan Grande, Poblacion District, Davao City, 8000, Philippines

rpespina@gmail.com
www.junespina.com

CONTENTS

INTRODUCTION

1. AN OVERVIEW OF A NON-BORN-AGAIN OR CARNAL LIFE

2. THE MISCONCEPTIONS ABOUT THE BORN-AGAIN EXPERIENCE

3. AN EXPOSITION OF THE BORN-AGAIN EXPERIENCE

4. PSEUDO-CHRISTIAN DISTINCTIVES

5. OF NOMINAL CHRISTIANITY

6. WHAT BORN AGAIN IS NOT?

7. WHAT BORN AGAIN IS?

8. NO LONGER A PHENOMENON

9. CHRIST'S ALLUSION FROM THE OLD TESTAMENT'S BRONZE SERPENT

10. THE KIND OF FAITH THAT LEADS TO THE SECOND BIRTH

11. THE ASSURANCE OF THE BORN-AGAIN BELIEVER

12. OUR DIVINE SONSHIP AS BORN-AGAIN CHRISTIANS

13. OF THE HYPER-CALVINIST'S HERESY

14. THE FUTURE OF THE BORN-AGAIN CHRISTIAN

15. CONCLUSION

ABOUT THE AUTHOR

ACKNOWLEDGMENTS

My humble understanding of fundamental doctrines grew—the Scriptures opened as with having a key that unlocks the door of the sacred writings—through the lives, books (or sermons) of many gifted born-again Christians. I am indebted to them whom the Holy Spirit used to equip me with the age-old teachings of Christian fundamentalism. Our dear Lord Jesus Christ gifted me with a good wife (my beloved Virgie) who understands my need for some precious waking hours alone in writing this book. I would always speak up for Jesus Christ, my Savior, and God. As a believer, all my circumstances work together to help me in this work. Paul once said: "[W]e . . . believe, therefore we . . . speak." (2 Cor. 4:13) Christ gave me this volume and sustained me, heart and soul—to Him be the glory.

Book Cover Image (Sunset) by Barbara Jackson from Pixabay.
Book Cover Design by Jun P. Espina.

DISCLAIMER

While we verify rigorously the information, citations, and references in this book, both the author and publisher make no representations or warranties of any kind, express or implied about the completeness, accuracy, reliability, suitability, or availability regarding all the internet-sourced information in this material. Any reliance you place on such information is therefore strictly at your own risk. Any perceived remark, comment, or use of organizations, people mentioned, and any resemblance to characters living, dead or otherwise, real or fictitious, is purely unintentional and used as examples only. Any perceived slights, misrepresentations, mischaracterizations of specific persons, peoples, or organizations, and/or published materials are unintentional and are intended solely for entertainment and informative value ONLY.

INTRODUCTION

MOST PEOPLE DISMISS Christ's message of our eternal life in heaven as it is too good a teaching to be true. Life after death is just beyond the radar of our earthly minds. People died, and no one returned to tell the story. It's how negative we are about the Gospel. For even though Christ resurrected, we persist in rejecting His Word.

It is the core of this book: "Born Again Christ's Version: Understanding the Biblical Born-Again Experience."

Wrote Charles Ryle: You may know how Christ "lived, and how He suffered, and how He died. But unless you know the power of Christ's cross by experience, — unless you know and feel within that the blood shed on that cross has washed away your own particular sins, — unless you are willing to confess that your salvation depends entirely on the work that Christ did upon the cross, — unless this be the case, Christ will profit you nothing. The mere knowing Christ's name will never save you."[1]

Thus, we need to know more about the born-again experience.

When someone tells you the path to longevity, you would love and follow him because you don't want to die. The grave terrifies us. But when the Son of God condescended to redeem us from sin by His death on the cross, the Jews crucified Him because He offered to all immortal bliss in God's city.

Christ loves us and wants us to be with Him in heaven, but we crucified Him daily in our hearts by unbelief.

This book, Born Again Christ's Version, presents the benefits of trusting and relying upon Christ's promises related

---

[1] J. C. Ryle, Old Paths (The Banner of Truth Trust, Edinburgh, U.K., First Published, 1878, Reprinted 2005), pp. 247-49.

to the unknown realm after death. It deals with the second birth experience according to the Word of God, as it is our Lord's method to live forever.

Nicodemus be born again to inherit God's kingdom. It was Christ's message over 2000 years ago.

We also offer a positive clue for those genuine believers of Christ, not only for the infants in the faith but also for the mature ones. And for the unbelievers, this paper aims to help them see the validity of Christ's promises given His resurrection from the dead.

Christ said we need to have a rebirth to live forever. He used the phrase "born again" to avoid the clutter of unnecessary doctrines on how to inherit eternal life. This paper intends to clarify further, by introducing a biblical survey of what is already as simple as two-word teaching.

We discuss here the misconceptions and the right view of the born-again experience.

May this little book help you in seeing the requirements of your entrance to heaven through the eye of the biblical second birth as required by Christ, our Lord.

1. AN OVERVIEW OF A NON-BORN-AGAIN OR CARNAL LIFE

*"But a natural man does not accept the things of
the Spirit of God, for they are foolishness to him."*
— 1 Corinthians 2:14.

I AM NOT a Christian," declared a former megachurch pastor, Joshua Harris, around twenty years after publishing his best-selling book, "I Kissed Dating Goodbye" in 1997. We heard many Christian leaders leaving Christianity and the primary reason is sin. Harris also left his wife, not just his faith.[2] Jim Bakker, a well-known televangelist, also spent years in jail as a fraudster.[3] According to the Bible, these leaders do not represent born-again Christian behavior.

What is a Carnal Life?

Carnal means flesh. It is the other term we used for the non-born-again existence. Our carnal life is the being we knew of since our birth. Without Christ's Spirit in our soul, we would leave this planet without understanding "the things of the Spirit of God." (1 Cor. 2:14) Our lack of love for our Creator and our ignorance of Him describe our carnal or godless existence. The born-again life we are examining in this book is just on the other side of the fence. The scriptural second

---

[2] Bote, Joshua. He wrote the Christian case against dating. Now he's splitting from his wife and faith. Usatoday.com. https://www.usatoday.com/story/news/nation/2019/07/29/joshua-harris-i-kissed-dating-goodbye-i-am-not-christian/1857934001/ (accessed May 4, 2020).

[3] https://en.wikipedia.org/wiki/Jim_Bakker

birth is different as night and day from the carnal life!

In his Epistle to the Galatians, the apostle Paul said, the "deeds of the flesh . . . are immorality, impurity, sensuality, idolatry, sorcery, enmities, strife, jealousy, outbursts of anger, disputes, dissensions, factions, envying, drunkenness, carousing, and things like these . . . those who practice such things will not inherit the kingdom of God." (Gal. 5:19-21)

Is there one man among us who is perfect, without experiencing anger, envy, jealousy, or sensuality? No one.

That is why Christ said, "[U]nless one is BORN AGAIN he cannot see the kingdom of God." (John 3:3) What's the point? Well, wrote the apostle John: "Jesus answered and said to [Nicodemus], 'Are you the teacher of Israel and do not understand these things?'" (John 3:10) Christ's train of thought at this moment with Nicodemus correlates with His teaching thirteen verses after, in the same Chapter Three of John, that God so loved "the world that He gave His only begotten Son, that whoever believes in Him shall not perish, but have eternal life." (John 3:16) Along with it, Christ rebuked Nicodemus' self-righteousness as an expert in God's written law and as a top Pharisee and defender of Judaism. Note the depth of Christ's question to Nicodemus: "Are you the teacher of Israel and do not understand these things?" Christ saw only spiritual blindness and ignorance in all those not experiencing the second birth irrespective of their religious scholarship and rank. And the root of this darkness is their belief in helping God save their soul through obeying the Law. Even the most ignorant man in the ditch has this belief system. He wants to help God save himself. Our Lord, however, taught that God so loved us that He gave His only begotten Son, Jesus, for us to get eternal life and the salvation of our souls by faith in the risen Christ alone. Sad that the carnal person does not understand that the born-again experience is the work of God's Spirit in the soul of those receiving Jesus in their hearts as only Savior, Lord, and God the Son.

From the teachings of our Lord Jesus, we learned the born-again experience as something separated from one's perfect obedience with God's Written Law. Christ even uncovered the ignorance of one Jewish legal expert, Nicodemus, in this matter. The second birth is the divine intervention of God's Spirit in the soul since God the Father loved us and gave His only Son Jesus for our Savior and Redeemer.

On the other side of the picture, the carnal mind just revolves around his five senses of seeing, hearing, smelling, touching, and tasting. The thought about God's giving His Son to die for our sins at Calvary doesn't cross his mind. The thought of trusting his soul and eternal future upon our risen Lord Jesus doesn't live in his heart. For him, death is just the end of the works of the five senses. Wrote one American screenwriter, David Gerrold: "Life is hard. Then you die. Then they throw dirt in your face. Then the worms eat you. Be grateful it happens in that order."[4] Well, it happens in the natural order of life, then death. But Christ said, if you are born again, the order of existence would be life, then physical death, then eternal life in heaven.

In the elbow room of the born-again experience, the natural and flesh-centered person is blind to the works of God's Spirit anyhow. The greatest minds who are not born-again Christians accept willingly this order of death in the grave after a life of less than 80 years, without regard for Christ's promised immortality in heaven. The former Philippine

---

4 David Gerrold Quotes. Brainyquote.com
https://www.brainyquote.com/quotes/david_gerrold_136980
(accessed January 21, 2021).

president, Corazon Aquino, once said, "I would rather die a meaningful death than to live a meaningless life." Death is the end of life, and that's all the carnal person clings to in the back of his mind.

The carnal life is not attentive to the things of the Spirit of God. For this, Paul said, "The person without the Spirit does not accept the things that come from the Spirit of God but considers them foolishness, and cannot understand them because they are discerned only through the Spirit." (1 Cor. 1:14, NIV) Our eternal life in heaven belongs to the Spirit of God. But the devil, our enemy, wants us to drift away from this truth forever until we get salvation by meeting Christ in our heart and experience the second birth by faith in His atoning blood.

Is There Such a Thing as the Spiritual Experience of the Carnal Life?

The natural man whom we also refer to as the carnal or flesh-centered person in this book may also meet a spiritual experience or event affecting the human spirit. For example, in First Kings, Chapter 18, we find the priests of Baal chanting with a loud voice, leaping and jumping and cutting themselves with a sword as they prayed for Baal's answer. (See First Kings 18:26-29) I met a cultic man, for another example, who shared to me a story about her daughter's answered prayers by praying before a female cult leader for hours. For thousands of years, myths and superstitions filled our literary archives as humanity recorded diverse spiritual encounters in all generations.

We can list down varied spiritual experiences — even the Muslims have their version of them! — but the biblical spirituality we are discussing here is beyond the sphere of the carnal life. Both Harris and Bakker, for example, have experienced a spiritual awakening of sorts as leaders and members of the Charismatic persuasion. But theirs is not the born-again experience we unriddle in this material.

In the Charismatic Movement, miracles, healing, speaking in tongues and other so-called "signs and wonders" are like treasured doctrines for its followers. But in Matthew 7, however, Christ said He didn't acknowledge as His own those miracle workers and healers during His time, an awful portent of the birth of extreme Pentecostalism. Will Christ own those Pentecostal healers, miracle workers, and tongue speakers who have changed tune and became so quiet as the grave at night during the COVID-19 pandemic?

Spiritualism in the district of superstition and myths floods humanity since the dawn of time. In Thailand, mind-blowing temples inspired a tsunami of tourists. Yes, these structures depict a high-level faith in Buddha. They prove the force of religion as an essential timber of human nature.

Voodooism, for another example, is very spiritual. It is about the spirit of the ancestors giving blessings. It also involves witchcraft and sorcery. We may write details of a thousand types of spirit worship or involvement in the lives of cult members, but they are not the born-again experience riveted in this paper.

What are the Expectations of the Carnal Life?

From the biblical viewpoint, the carnal life is devoid of hope. It does not expect any good at all in the afterlife. We find in Hebrews that the flesh-centered people "have lived their lives as slaves to the fear of dying." (Heb. 2:15, NLT)

The largest religious groups are Christianity (not the born-again Christianity!), Islam, Hinduism, Buddhism, the Unaffiliated (the irreligious and atheist) groups, and the Folk Religion. Multitudes have aligned themselves with any of these doctrinal groups. But none of these billions of people have the living hope of life with God forever in heaven as taught by Christ.

The Koranic paradise is sensual (it's about wives, 72 virgins—all this sexual madness!) and is destitute of holiness and divinity characteristic of the heaven as described by Christ. In Matthew, our Lord taught that "in the resurrection they neither marry nor are given in marriage, but are like angels in heaven." (Matt. 22:30)

In Hinduism, the Hindus taught about the endless rebirth of the soul known as the reincarnation until reaching Moksha, which is the end of the death and rebirth cycle. A serious study of this teaching would only reveal the shining face of carnality, which is the overcoming of ignorance and desires. This doctrine mentions just the material side of man, but not the resurrected body and glorious immortality in the city of God of the born-again believer of Christ.

What are the expectations of the carnal life? Well, the non-born-again existence only expects death and hopelessness while waiting for the last breath.

The atheist Stephen Hawking, for example, said, "Before we understand science, it is natural to believe that God created the universe. But now science offers a more convincing explanation." Since Hawking's science cannot guarantee life after death, it is logical to assume he died a hopeless man—a man expecting nothing after this life.

Can you imagine a genius like Hawking declaring death as no different from a computer being turned off? Is not death equivalent to just fading into the night like Batman and then to nothingness? No moral responsibility at all to the God who created us?

Christ said we need spiritual rebirth to see the things of

God.

Wrote the apostle Paul: It "is written, 'THINGS WHICH EYE HAS NOT SEEN AND EAR HAS NOT HEARD, AND which HAVE NOT ENTERED THE HEART OF MAN, ALL THAT GOD HAS PREPARED FOR THOSE WHO LOVE HIM.'" (1 Cor. 2:9)

The carnal mind is just like the huge diamond stored in the bowels of the earth. He cannot see or hear the things of God. The promises of our Creator don't have a chance in dousing his heart. Like the precious stone, Satan hides his soul in the peaks and valleys of darkness.

We were like a blind man to everything biblical before our second birth event. I experienced it before my conversion. According to the apostle Paul, the reason is "you were at that time separate from Christ . . . having no hope and without God in the world." (Eph. 2:12)

A carnal person does not have hope of immortality and resurrection from the grave, and he is also godless. He is without hope and without God in the world, according to the Bible.

Name your religion, but if you don't have hope of life after death, then that faith of yours is not born-again Christianity. When death comes, Christ cannot welcome you in heaven. You don't know Him, and meeting Him is as impossible as expecting the smile of the God you don't worship in your lifetime. The carnal life ends in death. The second life in heaven is not a part of it since rebirth is required to live forever. Unless a man is born again, to quote Christ again, no one can enter God's kingdom.

The flesh-centered person has zero confidence in the great beyond. But it is not the most alarming cancer of his spiritual condition. Rather, it is the naked truth that the devil blinded him. His soul's salvation is never a part of his goals in this life.

Who is the God of the Carnal Life?

Who was your God before you became a born-again believer of Christ? The genuine Catholic may answer, "I pray to Mother Mary"; while the orthodox Jew would say, "I pray to the living God of Abraham." "I pray to Allah," a Muslim would quip confidently. In my experience, I cried for help from an unknown God since I was more uncatholic in my inherited Catholicism. Before my conversion and second birth experience, I prayed instinctively to a god I didn't know who. I grew up listening to my grandmother's novena in mixed Spanish and Latin. It sometimes sounds like "speaking in tongues" for me. I was sure my grandma didn't understand it, too. It was a religious exercise of sorts that taught me nothing about who to worship. The Bible taught that faith in a god is part of human nature. But who that God is?

Is it true that we gave different names to the same God? No. It is not.

Our Lord Jesus enlightens all people concerning His Father, God, since He is the light of the world. It is a Bible teaching in John 1:9, specifically, not to mention other related Scriptures. Paul also wrote that knowledge about God is clear within us, so we are without excuse. (Rom. 1:18-23) I experienced preaching before a handful of old people where they protested, alleging I didn't have evidence about the Gospel I shared with them. My evidence was the Bible and Jesus Christ, the Son of God, who once walked on this planet. He died on the cross and rose from the grave. The Scriptures and the annals of written history proved our Lord's earthly life. The natural and carnal people, however, cannot process these things because they cannot pick up what is true from the God of the Holy Scriptures. In Matthew 13, Christ said: "And in their case the prophecy of Isaiah is being fulfilled, which says, You shall keep on listening, but shall not understand; And you shall keep on looking, but shall not perceive." (v. 14)

A Chinese friend showed me one of his new arrivals from China. It was a beautiful Chinese goddess for business carved in Jade. I didn't know who it was. Perhaps she was Quan Yin, the goddess of mercy for the Buddhists. Then, I asked my friend, "can she hear our prayers?" He was silent, unwilling to assert his faith so as not to degrade his reputation as a former professor in Hong Kong. The carnal person is always unsure of his god or goddess.

But who is God? Well, He is the Father of Christ, and you cannot find Him without encountering Christ's Spirit first in your heart by believing. In John 14:23, "Jesus answered and said to him, 'If anyone loves Me, he will follow My word; and My Father will love him, and We will come to him and make Our dwelling with him.'" The Father will come to you only if you have the Savior, Jesus, in your heart. God cannot accept you and your sinful soul on the grounds of His perfect holiness. Hence, Christ claimed He is the Way to the Father because He died as a ransom for our sins. Second, He also said: "Blessed are the pure in heart, for they will see God." In short, blessed are those forgiven believers by faith in our Lord's redemptive work at Calvary. Finally, God is Spirit, and "does not dwell in temples made by hands." (Acts 17:24) In sum, the non-born-again person believes in idols made of wood and other types of deity because he does not have the God of the Scriptures, the Father of Christ. He is a lost soul needing salvation by faith in Christ's substitutionary death.

When Jesus rebuked Peter, He said: "Get behind Me, Satan! You are a stumbling block to Me; for you are not setting your mind on God's interests, but man's." (Matt. 16:23) The non-born-again life is always like that. Day in and day out, his mind and heart entertain only the things that concern his material being and needs. He does not love our Father God because he rejects Jesus. He is out of God's range in terms of the Father-and-child relationship as taught in the Scriptures. The devil taught Adam and Eve that disobedience to their Creator can deliver them from God's version of right and wrong. "For God knows," said Satan, "that in the day you eat from it your eyes will be opened, and you will be like God, knowing good and evil." (Gen. 3:5)

As a result, man invented his own gods, for he knows what is right and wrong. God's Word mentioned Baal, Molech, Diana among other gods and goddesses worshipped by the ancient peoples of the world. The Greeks worshipped Ares, their god of war, while the Hindus adored Parvati, their goddess of fertility. Yes, the carnal man cooks up his own gods as a lost soul, and cheers up with that, like a hungry man enjoying the wrong nourishment, since the heavenly Father wired his nature up with a craving for Someone Bigger. He knows he needs God, but he went astray because Jesus is the only Way to the Father, and our Lord does not know him as His own child. Christ's Spirit is not in his soul. He is not born of God. Said the apostle John, "By this we know that we remain in Him and He in us, because He has given to us of His Spirit." (1 John 4:13) Christ indwells the genuine born-again Christian. But the carnal man knows nothing about such a bond since he is an unsaved soul. The most pitiful person in the world, therefore, is one who's surfing tons of information from the Internet but still ignorant about heaven and eternal life by faith in Jesus.

The carnal or non-born-again life is synonymous with a worldly existence, with no semblance of love for our Maker, our Lord Jesus, and the things spiritual and eternal. Paul said, "we look . . . at the things which are not seen; for the things which are seen are temporal, but the things which are not seen are eternal." (2 Cor. 4:18) The carnal life is different. His gods' roles and works always go with the flow of his survival. The things of the Scriptures don't impress him. We heard about the god of fishing, the god of war, or the goddess of fertility. It is how the carnal god behaves and functions from the horse sense of the flesh-focused people. It's all about the material side of things!

The quotes and statements from the atheists published on the Internet reveal how they worship research, science, philosophy, and reason. For example, George Carlin, a stand-up comedian and atheist, once said he worshipped the sun because it gave him "heat, light, food, and a lovely day." The carnal man limits the works and powers of his invented gods to the material affairs of his sojourn on the earth. After mocking religion and Christianity, Carlin preached his sun god, feeling superior to his twisted logic of turning the hand of time seven centuries backward—during the worship of Aten, the sun god of the Egyptians in the 14th century. It's like science turned upside down.

The devil stupefied billions of people to thwart God's redemption plan. Through King Herod, Satan ordered (but failed) to murder the young Jesus. Then wrote the apostle Paul concerning Satan's deception: "If the Good News we preach is hidden behind a veil, it is hidden only from people who are perishing." (2 Cor. 4:3, NLT)

The carnal or non-born-again people worship a flesh-engaging deity because they are hell-bound and Satan-blinded. Jesus said, "Come to Me." This is Christ's invitation. I listened to His call and got saved. I pray you will obey Him, too.

What Happens After the Death of the Carnal Life?

We don't have enough information about the death experience, except the NDE (Near Death Experience) database. In these experiences, people saw patterns depending on religious persuasion. The Hindu guy has his experience from his belief system, just as the Christian has his hell, heaven, angels, and Jesus visions.

The biblical account about death is the most definitive account of the death experience. Christ gave a parable about "The Rich Man and Lazarus." "Now the poor man died," said our Lord, "and was carried away by the angels to Abraham's bosom; and the rich man also died and was buried." (Luke 16:22) In one verse, we find the born-again Christian (Lazarus) "carried away by the angels to Abraham's bosom." Why we have a truth claim that Lazarus was a born-again Christian? The answer is that he went to Abraham's bosom (or he went to heaven). We are sure of it because Jesus said that Abraham is alive because God Himself said, "I am the God of Abraham," which means, "He is not the God of the dead but of the living." (Matt. 22:32b)

Second, we are sure Lazarus was born again, because Christ said, "Truly, truly, I say to you, unless one is born again he cannot see the kingdom of God." (John 3:3) Now we see: Lazarus went to heaven!

The Rich Man in the parable also died and was buried. Hence his death was real. The burial happened. But no services from the angels who carried Lazarus to God's home.

The death of the carnal people does not involve so much divine surge, unlike the death of the genuine believer in Jesus. The reason is that God takes "no pleasure in the death of the wicked." (Ezek. 33:11) The Rich Man went to hell as fast as

Lazarus celebrated eternal life in the presence of God. "In Hades," according to the parable, "he lifted up his eyes, being in torment, and saw Abraham far away and Lazarus in his bosom." (Luke 19:23)

How did it happen that Lazarus becomes a believer, unlike the Rich Man? The answer is that Lazarus desired `the crumbs from the Rich Man's table and the dogs came and licked his sores. (Cf. Luke 16:20-21) Lazarus' God was so real to him, his relationship with his Creator sealed like no other man alive given his predicament. It is Christianity 101. "I am the vine," taught Christ, "you are the branches; he who abides in Me and I in him, he bears much fruit, for apart from Me you can do nothing." (John 15:5) In the second birth experience, faith in Christ involves trust. Genuine trust!

The Rich Man could not have the *Lazarusian* faith because of his abundance. Taught Christ about the rich man who told his soul to "take your ease, eat, drink and be merry." But God said to him "'You fool! This very night your soul is required of you; and now who will own what you have prepared?' So is the man who stores up treasure for himself, and is not rich toward God." (Luke 12:19)

Are we teaching that wealth is awful and poverty, virtuous? A big no!

What we are expounding is the miracle of the born-again experience. Heaven is not about money or poverty. It is about spiritual rebirth, which can happen upon the soul only by faith in Jesus as the Savior and Lord of all. For "with the heart a person believes, resulting in righteousness, and with the mouth he confesses, resulting in salvation." (Rom. 10:10)

Before we close this chapter, let us refresh ourselves with the core Scripture in this book:

Jesus answered and said to him, "Truly, truly, I say to you,

unless one is born again he cannot see the kingdom of God."
(John 3:3)

How to Save the Carnal Life?

If you are unsaved, you are a carnal person needing the second birth experience to live forever in heaven. First, you need to believe Christ's teaching that "unless one is born again he cannot see the kingdom of God." You must first meet God's Spirit in your soul in this life to have eternal life after death. It is a problem, but we can fix it if we acknowledge the second birth as the only path to immortality. Paul said, "[Y]ou are not in the flesh but in the Spirit, if indeed the Spirit of God dwells in you." (Rom. 8:9a) Without Christ Spirit in your soul, you are carnal and godless. (Rom. 8:9b; Eph. 2:12)

You need to have a born-again experience if you want eternal life. Born again means born of the Spirit of God, and you are not born of God if you are unsaved. Should God demand your soul today, you could only go straight toward hell as a man who is unrepentant, sinful, unforgiven, and without God's Spirit in your inner self. Are we sure of hell for the unsaved? Yes, Christ teaches it. He is the Truth and proves all His teachings by His resurrection. Observe John 3:18: "The one who believes in Him is not judged; the one who does not believe has been judged already, because he has not believed in the name of the only Son of God."

Are we sure to enter heaven if we are born again? Yes, Christ taught it, too.

How to get salvation and forgiveness and encounter the second birth event in life? Let's turn to the Word of God for an incontestable answer.

Paul said to Titus that God "saved us, not on the basis of deeds which we have done in righteousness, but according to His mercy, by the washing of regeneration and renewing by the Holy Spirit, whom He poured out upon us richly through Jesus Christ our Savior." (Titus 3:5) Our own deeds of righteousness, our good moral standing, and our benevolence, thoughtfulness, and sacrifices for the benefit of the world cannot save our soul from God's wrath because of sin. God won't save us based on the "deeds which we did in righteousness." It is the first point, and we've waxed on this teaching incessantly in this paper, lest the devil would steal it from your heart. You cannot save yourself and you cannot help God save yourself, according to the Scriptures.

Second, God sees your salvation as the "washing of regeneration and renewing by the Holy Spirit," and we cannot change what God thought it is. The rendering of Titus 3:5 (the Scripture we use) in NLT is clearer: God "washed away our sins, giving us a new birth and new life through the Holy Spirit." The born-again experience is about God's regeneration or restoration of us by giving us a new heart, a new spirit, and a new view about the eternal dangers of sin and Christ's condescension to ransom us from sin's penalty, which is the second death in hell.

How did God complete the salvation process of our souls? Well, He richly poured out upon us the Holy Spirit through Jesus Christ our Savior. In John 16:7, Christ said, "but if I go, I will send Him [the Holy Spirit] to you." In short, God cannot save you without Christ Jesus, our Redeemer, and Lord. God said, your salvation depends on Jesus! It is said in 1 John 1:2: "And if anyone sins, we have an Advocate [or Intercessor] with the Father, Jesus Christ the righteous; and He Himself is the propitiation [or satisfaction] for our sins." We are sinners and only Christ can offer us forgiveness and bring us closer to the Father.

Now, have you considered inviting the Spirit of the resurrected Jesus Christ into your heart to forgive and save you? God's Word in John, Chapter 1, gives us more detailed information on how to receive our Lord:

Jesus "came to His own, and those who were His own did not receive Him. But as many as received Him, to them He gave the right to become children of God, even to those who believe in His name, who were born, not of blood nor of the will of the flesh nor of the will of man, but of God." (Vv. 11-13)

Have you experienced believing in Jesus already? Yes, everybody does. Even the Muslims and the Hindus believe that the evidence about Christ is just so overwhelming and no one can deny His earthly life.

Hence, God added one requirement to get salvation, and that is to receive Christ into our hearts. Believing is not enough. Your right to divine sonship would take place only after receiving Jesus. "But as many as received Him, to them He gave the right to become children of God." Christ is God's Gift. (John 3:16; Rom. 6:23) But you can refuse that Gift. For example, God promised to the Israelites a gift of the land flowing with milk and honey. But they refused it and demanded Moses would send them back to Egypt. They refused the gift.

This very moment, Christ is knocking at the door of your heart. Your every heartbeat is life-giving, and that heartbeat is Christ Himself knocking on your door since He said, "I am the Life." You just don't invite Him, even though He presented Himself as a loving God the Son, who died to redeem us from the curse of sin. He even presented Himself as our loving Savior. In Revelation 3:20, Christ said, "Behold, I stand at the door and knock; if anyone hears My voice and opens the door, I will come in to him and will dine with him, and he with Me." You must receive Him as your only Lord, Savior, and God the Son or you will not see the kingdom of God.

I heard people claim they have believed and received

Christ, but nothing happened. Well, Judas did not just receive but also kissed Jesus. It is like believing in the gift, receiving it, but not appreciating it as the gift of eternal life. Paul said, "For the wages of sin is death, but the free gift of God is eternal life in Christ Jesus our Lord." (Rom. 6:23) But do we really believe it as the very Word of God? I do. The free gift of God is eternal life in Christ Jesus our Lord.

Wrote the apostle Paul in First Thessalonians 2:13: "For this reason we also constantly thank God that when you received the word of God which you heard from us, you accepted it not as the word of men, but for what it really is, the word of God, which also performs its work in you who believe." You are not saved because you don't take the Word of God seriously, just like Adam and Eve who rejected their Creator's warning not to eat the forbidden fruit. The word of God will only perform its work in you who believe. If nothing happened with you after having believed and received Christ into your heart, then the Word of God did not perform its work in you because your faith is superficial, just like the devil's faith that does not have the element of trust in it. D. L. Moody was one of the greatest evangelists and his last word was: "Is this dying? Why this is bliss. There is no valley, I have been within the gates. Earth is receding; Heaven is opening; God is calling; I must go." God used Moody like no other because the Father's Word performed its work with Moody.

For another illustration, the first European convert named Lydia, who was a worshipper of God, listened "and the Lord opened her heart to respond to the things spoken by Paul." (Acts 16:14) She got saved because Lydia had a God-thirsty soul (she was a worshipper of God) and when she listened to the Gospel, God opened her heart and saved her.

You can be born again if you think you need God's offer of free salvation from God's judgment by faith in Christ. If you don't need it, you don't deserve to be with Jesus and the angels of God in heaven forever. You don't praise God, much less appreciate Christ's atoning blood.

Ask for salvation and the Spirit of God by faith in Jesus as Savior and Lord and you will be saved. Your carnal self will disappear as you meet the born-again experience.

Life's terrible failure is not the lack of food or good health but the lack of the Holy Spirit in the soul and the absence of assurance of eternal life after death.

2. THE MISCONCEPTIONS ABOUT THE BORN-AGAIN EXPERIENCE

"Having the appearance of godliness, but denying its power. Avoid such people." — 2 Timothy 3:5.

THE APOSTLE PAUL wrote that godliness is power (2 Tim. 3:5) because it is a connection to Jesus Christ who has all rule and authority in heaven and on earth. (Matt. 28:18) But, as Christians, Paul told us to avoid the ungodly Christians—the impostors! These guys have a semblance of religious enthusiasm, but they are not born-again Christians. They don't have Christ's Spirit in their souls!

First Misconception: It is Not Christian Enthusiasm

I experienced buying many Christian books from a pastor who studied in the United States. (He sold the books he purchased while in the US.) After a year, I noticed the guy mastered argumentation and debate without regard for holiness. You cannot see in him any love for Jesus. Paul said, "Avoid such people." Given his questionable Christianity, I didn't buy his books again. "This edition is no longer sold in the market." He got down cold on his sales presentation, but I went to the internet instead for my love for books.

He became powerless to influence me because of his resolve to humanize the things of God and rationalize them instead to win an argument. Ungodliness is powerlessness—even if you have thousands of excellent books in your library! "Having the appearance of godliness," wrote the apostle Paul, "but denying its power. Avoid such people."

We cannot always equate Christian enthusiasm with born-again Christianity.

Second Misconception: It is Not Pretension of Godliness

I met a friend way back in the early 1990s who helped me gain a farmland. One day he said, "Friend, this area I am selling spreads by the road; you can spit on the National Highway." But what I disliked about this guy's rhetoric is his habit of starting his sentence with "My beloved God," as if he is enjoying his pretended godliness. I am sure of his fake Christianity after he shared his story about how he killed a man mercilessly. Then he fled away and married a landed widow who had eight children. His life stuck around a war zone with his wife's children. He cursed—unveiling his mountains of hatred toward his wife's children—then ended his string of expletives with the phrase "my beloved God." My friend was an unbeliever, and I saw the face of his unbelief firsthand. The genuine born-again Christians won't use the name of the Lord in vain. (Ex. 20:7) They differ from those rejecters of Christ Jesus in the space of moral discernment.

My friend suffered from an acute godly pretension disorder, but such slimy hypocrisy is not born-again Christianity.

Pretended Christianity contradicts the born-again experience. When you understand that salvation is free, you don't need hypocrisy; you don't need a scared-rabbit behavior to gladden your fellowship. Just grab your eternal life like one hungry for the truth by believing it comes from our Lord Jesus for free!

But if your desire is Church acceptance, then you are pretending, and Christ cannot find your heart loaded with faith upon Him.

If you don't love Jesus, then you mistrust Him. You are not born again—and you're extremely far away from God!

No fake godliness can survive in born-again Christianity. Some pastors and leaders left the faith after trying hard to behave like genuine children of God. The charlatans in the church are restless, having no indwelling Holy Spirit. Their best option is to leave, then charge the Christians as exclusionists and bigots.

We cannot put godliness on the far side of our born-again existence since it is about our attitude toward Jesus under the control of God's Spirit. I used to ask my children this question after a Sunday worship service: "Did the preacher mention Jesus in his sermon?" Can you imagine a preacher delivering a Christless sermon for one hour?

We cannot stay godly outside of Christ's glorification. The apostle Peter said that Christ granted to us everything pertaining to life and godliness. (1 Peter 1:1-3)

The born-again experience spins around Christ's honor and exaltation, and no doctrinal preciseness or superiority can alter that truth.

Third Misconception: It is Not Fear toward God

The genuine Christians have two things in common which the rejecters of Christ couldn't fathom. First, Christ's children don't fear death, and second, they don't fear God. Before John Knox died, he said, "Live in Christ, live in Christ, and the flesh need not fear death." The unbelievers tremble at the prospect of dying out of fear of meeting our most Holy Father in heaven. The fear of God and the fear of death just work together like two sides of the same table. But the born-again Christians don't share the same perturbation. Paul taught that while we were still sinners, Christ died for us; while we were still enemies with God, Christ shed His own blood and died to clothe us with divine forgiveness and reconciliation. (Rom. 5:8-11) No longer do I call you slaves, Christ said, but friends. (Cf. John 15:15)

Through their faith in Jesus, the born-again Christians are friends with God. (Cf. Jas. 2:23)

The Old Testament taught about the fear of God, which would always terrify the hearts of all Israelites every time they would disobey God during the Exodus. Then Moses would come and intercede for them. In the born-again experience, it is the love of Jesus that describes our relationship with our Father God. Taught the Scriptures in Hebrews 7:25: "Therefore He is also able to save forever those who come to God through Him, since He always lives to make intercession for them."

To bring to light one's fear toward God, let's examine the Muslim belief system. Allah's arbitrary will and dominion represent the compendium of his alleged divine attributes. He is untouchable and incapable of a personal and loving relationship with his followers. Islam means submission to Allah. Since he is not a father to the believers, love therefore, is not a part of Allah's nature.

It is the core of all fanatical belief systems. Fear. Yes, fear of the gods' displeasure and retribution!

One can be a devout Muslim, for example, out of fear of Allah's anger, and not out of love for Allah's concern for the soul.

Born-again Christianity does not work like that. It is about love, and not terror as this Quranic verse proves: "Soon shall We cast terror into the hearts of the Unbelievers." (Quran 3:151)

The basic principle behind the scriptural Christian life is the love of God in the framework of freedom—not via fear or slavery because God is love. I submitted myself to a water baptism and church membership, for example, from the paradigm of liberty. I received Christ as my personal Lord and Savior from my complete freedom of choice, and not through the ISIS-style of evangelism at gunpoint.

Like Islamism, the Crusades and the Inquisition were nothing more than Christianization under threat. They were not God's campaigns, obviously.

In born-again Christianity, however, the emphasis is on the fatherhood of God, and with it His love to Christ's followers. Taught our Lord: "I ascend to My Father and your Father, and My God and your God." (John 20:17b) Freedom is necessary to genuine love. If you would force a woman to love you, for example, you could go to prison as a rapist. Our holy life flows out of our freeness to love our Creator.

With freedom, fear cannot thrive!

The Christian scriptural doctrine is easy to grasp. We were enemies with God because of sin, and fear of our Creator is a natural experience for every one of us. We sometimes describe it as the fear of the unknown Supreme Being. But with the born-again experience, our heart would always rest on the Bible truth that, "God has not destined us for wrath, but for obtaining salvation through our Lord Jesus Christ." (1 Thess. 5:9)

A Christian who fears God and death like the unbeliever is a confused religious person without a second birth experience.

Fourth Misconception: It is Not Compulsion

It happened in many Christian families. Their young behaved like Christians to please their parents. A man having ten children, for example, attended church late—always late! The pastor asked him why. "Before her death," he replied, "my wife told me never to miss church attendance." Compulsion or anything contrary to freedom of choice is not born again in Christianity. We can only worship in freedom, not at gunpoint. The early Christians met in caves to worship Jesus unrestrained.

When we pray, we do so out of our faith and affection to our risen Jesus. Our holiness, therefore, fuses with our love for Christ. And there is no love without the plethora of freedom to love.

Wrote Paul: "Now the Lord is the Spirit, and where the Spirit of the Lord is, there is liberty." (2 Cor. 3:17) "So if the Son makes you free, you will be free indeed," said John. (John 8:36) Since I have the freedom to follow and love Christ, my Lord will intercede for me (Cf. Rom. 8:34), since freedom also involves the choice to sin. Ravi Zacharias said that freedom to love entails God's sending to us the Savior.

Wrote the apostle Paul, "If anyone does not love the Lord, he is to be accursed." (1 Cor. 16:22) And in Galatians 5:1, Paul clearly stressed his teaching about Christian liberty: "It was for freedom that Christ set us free; therefore, keep standing firm and do not be subject again to a yoke of slavery." We based our godly life on the freedom given us to love, obey, and live a sanctified life. We don't live the Christian life under threat or for fear the church will expel us from our membership.

Most religious cults' core teachings set up on the precept of disfellowshipping. They weaponize membership expulsion to advance their camaraderie-focused and love-our-group doctrines. What they lack is Jesus. Their ways don't stand for the born-again experience.

The born-again Christian loves Christ naturally because the Spirit of God dwells in him. (Read Rom. 8:9) "We love, because He first loved us." (1 John 4:19)

No compulsion prospers in genuine born-again Christianity.

Fifth Misconception: It is Not Avoidance of Christ

Unbelief has so many faces. I knew of a church pastor who scarcely mentions the name of Jesus Christ in his sermons except the tired "in the name of Jesus" before closing a prayer. He structured his sermon outlines well. His message was biblical, except that Christ's glory was not the center of his messages. The New Testament writers composed their write-ups around Christ, even spanning across the error of redundancy in the eyes of the modern grammarians. Observe 1 Corinthians 1:1-4:

> 1 Paul, called as an apostle of Jesus Christ by the will of God, and Sosthenes our brother,

> 2 To the church of God which is at Corinth, to those who have been sanctified in Christ Jesus, saints by calling, with all who in every place call on the name of our Lord Jesus Christ, their Lord and ours:

> 3 Grace to you and peace from God our Father and the Lord Jesus Christ.

> 4 I thank my God always concerning you for the grace of God which was given you in Christ Jesus. (1 Cor. 1:1-4)

In four verses comprising 90 words in NASB, Paul mentioned: "Jesus Christ" or "Christ Jesus" five times since he cited our Lord on every verse and twice in verse two. Jesus Christ is two words or ten words for the name of our Lord in a 90-word composition. Well, it is 11.11% of the 4-verse note. It is redundant, right? Paul could use "He" or the Son or our Lord to break a monotonous rhythm. Instead, he used "Jesus

Christ" five times in four short verses. Unbelief, on the other hand, hides Christ. The word "God" is the common replacement among careless Bible lecturers instead of Christ or Jesus Christ.

The so-called "Muslim Obama," for example, imposed "Happy Holidays" instead of "Merry Christmas" to erase the significance of Christ's birth. It is another face of unbelief. During his US presidency, homosexuality is a top priority—another offense to biblical Christianity!

Avoidance of Christ is not born again in Christianity.

I used to attend Bible classes after the worship service. I noticed some are born-again Christians; others are not. There is a problem since everyone believes they are Christians. Those who are not truly born-again believers of Christ insist that they too are bona fide church members, and therefore, followers of Christ. As a student of unbelief, I observe that those faking their church membership don't have a sound Bible teaching or doctrine in their hearts. They are silent, and when they take part in the discussions, they show only ignorance and emptiness. They are avoiding Christ!

Sixth Misconception: It is Not Insensitivity to Sound Doctrines

Around nine years after my conversion, I left the first Christian group that led me to Christ and became an independent worker of our Lord. I told the pastor who baptized me I was leaving since I don't believe our assembly was the only genuine Church of Jesus, and our baptism, the only allowed version. My church friends persuaded me to stay since my objection was just a trivial doctrinal issue. I didn't listen and as a result, lost all my friends from that fellowship. Can you imagine the struggle I faced, serving Jesus alone as a preacher, for the sake of teaching only sound doctrines?

Said Spurgeon that God won't work with a teacher teaching his denomination's heresy instead of teaching the truth from the Scriptures through the Holy Spirit's guidance. The so-called legit baptism of the group, according to this false teaching, adds the born-again Christian to the Lord's Church, meaning their assembly taught there is no other true church, except theirs. As I studied the Bible, I bumped into Acts 2:47, which states that "the Lord was adding to their number day by day those who were being saved." It is our Lord who was adding the saved members to His body, the Church, not the pastor or his baptism! From it, God made firm my conviction. I need sound doctrines more than a thousand friends from a controversial assembly.

From the Christian groups, including the Christian cults, we find various heresies or false teachings.

The craze for signs and wonders, miracles, faith healing, and prosperity doctrines, for example, have put extreme Pentecostalism on the class of Christian denominations insensitive to sound doctrines. Wrote Paul in First Timothy 4 and verse one: "But the Spirit explicitly says that in later times some will fall away from the faith, paying attention to deceitful spirits and doctrines of demons." (I have a separate eBook on extreme Pentecostalism.) Christ said God teaches the born-again Christian, for the Spirit will teach him all things. (John 6:45; 14:26) "As for you," wrote the apostle John, "the anointing which you received from Him abides in you, and . . . His anointing teaches you about all things." (1 John 2:27) The Holy Spirit living in the truly saved Christian's soul will not be happy with the Pentecostals' rolling on the ground or the church's floor and "laughing with the Spirit." These abnormal Pentecostal stuff posted on Facebook came from the so-called Christianity of people insensitive to sound doctrines.

Paul taught Titus to "speak the things which are fitting for sound doctrine." (Tit. 2:1) In Jude 1:3, we find this Scripture "appealing that you contend earnestly for the faith which was once for all handed down to the saints." We need to defend the faith unless we are heartless for the solid biblical teachings which toughen those born of God.

The Christian cults like the Jehovah's Witness, the Iglesia ni Cristo (Church of Christ), the Church of the Latter-day Saints (Mormons), the Seventh-day Adventist (SDA), among others, have common doctrinal issues against born-again Christianity like the deity of Christ, the Gospel (that Christ died to redeem us from sin!), the Holy Trinity, salvation by faith alone and other scriptural and fundamental teachings.

One common mark of born-again Christians is their sensitivity to sound doctrines. If you ordered beef from the menu, for example, and got served with rat meat instead and you don't know the difference, it is because you don't understand things. The born-again Christian, however, is sensitive to the spiritual menu and would leave the unscriptural assembly quickly, like one fleeing from poisoned food.

I met two Doctors of Theology from South Korea who surveyed our place for their planned theological seminary. We shared Bible concepts and the books we read, and they gave me a bitter laugh when I mentioned Henry Clarence Theissen and his book, "Lectures on Systematic Theology." One of them then commented I read some peanuts. All the while, I learned they were from the crowd of the anti-Bible Liberal Theology.

Have you heard of Christian congregations ordaining LGBT female pastors? The Bible said, "no female pastors," but the Liberals don't believe that. Second, the Bible said homosexuals cannot enter the kingdom of God. The Liberals hate that, too!

Insensitivity to sound doctrines is, therefore, not a born-again Christian behavior.

3. AN EXPOSITION OF THE BORN-AGAIN EXPERIENCE

I will put My Spirit within you and cause you to walk in My statutes, and you will be careful to observe My ordinances. — Ezekiel 36:27.

The Salvation of the Soul is a Definite Born-Again Experience

WE NEED TO experience the second birth, or we will die in hell forever. The value of Christ's born-again precept, therefore, is just boundless. Our salvation from hell is bigger than the worth of the entire world. (Matt. 16: 26) Our spiritual rebirth is as priceless as our immortal soul. The good news is that we can have a definite experience of our salvation, which we also referred to in this paper as the born-again experience. We would know we are saved, just as God allowed Judas to know he was not.

If God would help me walk in His statutes and ordinances, it would be a distinct something. (See Ezek. 36:27)

Christ also uses the blowing of the wind as an illustration of the born-again phenomenon. (John 3:7-8) With it, it is impossible to speculate that the born-again requirement is just a doctrinal statement without sensing the newness it brings.

When John the Baptist's father, Zacharias, prophesied about him, he said:

"And you, child . . . give to His people the knowledge of salvation By the forgiveness of their sins." (Luke 1:76-78a)

Zacharias's teaching is clear. After experiencing forgiveness, Christ's people would know their salvation.

Paul also said that God "desires all men to be saved and to come to the knowledge of the truth." (1 Tim. 2:4) If you are saved, you would know you are—you would know the truth!

Over 20 years ago, I had an employee, a Pentecostal guy who told me his pastor taught him no one is assured of heaven, but in his heart, he was sure he had eternal life. He experienced a newness of life, and he knew it.

Yes, our salvation is a definite born-again experience.

Let's clarify our point. Salvation is not baptism or good works or knowledge about Christ or church membership. Wrote C. H. Spurgeon: "I do not ask you whether you are a Wesleyan, a Baptist, or a Presbyterian: my only question is, "Are you born again?"

The second birth is about the kind of faith in Jesus, which could lead to a genuine born-again experience. You may know Christ, even memorize verses about Him, without experiencing forgiveness and confidence of your immortality. A truly born-again person is a transformed individual spiritually, and he knows it.

When I got saved, I knew it. My immediate boss told me I had an after-baptism hangover. Later, I learned she was a lesbian Christian and had a wife. She mocked at my conversion because she had not experienced my Spirit-caused second birth.

For an added illustration, someone told me he wants to preach and serve the church. Fine, I replied. But you cannot have eternal life by doing that. You cannot enter God's kingdom because you are a pastor or a choir member. You must be a born-again disciple of Christ if you want eternal life!

That said, we can even close the entire Bible to underscore this teaching and just keep John 3 and verse 3 to get to the bottom of true Christianity, which is the second birth or the born-again experience.

The second birth is the indisputable path to eternal life, and it is experiential because it is about Christ's Spirit in our soul. (Rom. 8:9b)

God does not hide one's second birth event in life. When Christ's Spirit comes to forgive and live in your soul, you would know that God has possessed you, just as when some lower spirits bewitch an evil person. There would be an encounter; there would be fresh details of reality to see and witness.

Salvation is not something outside of the sphere of our experience.

That is why we can explain Paul's teaching that the born-again person is a new creature. That is why we can understand why Stephen, the first Christian martyr, faced martyrdom to defend his faith, instead of denying Jesus and run away. (2 Cor. 5:17; Acts 7:54-60) He experienced the divine peace and joy of a saved soul.

The Holy Spirit is Involved in the Born-Again Experience

I met many Bible-literate individuals who are not born again. Some of them are pastors and deacons. We had a highly active Sunday school teacher, for example, who suddenly disappeared from church attendance, left his wife, and returned to gambling. He was well-read, even guessing our ancestry by the types of our hair. (We have varied hair types because of colonization for almost 400 years.) These active fake Christians have earned the respect of the church somehow, but they are unforgiven sinners and should be removed from the leadership to preserve the church's doctrine and purity.

How to know that this guy claiming Christianity is fake? Well, easy. He is not born again. Remember that the second birth is an experience of a new heart and mind. Note this Word of God through the prophet Ezekiel:

Then I will sprinkle clean water on you, and you will be clean; I will cleanse you from all your filthiness and from all your idols. Moreover, I will give you a new heart and put a new spirit within you; and I will remove the heart of stone from your flesh and give you a heart of flesh. And I will put My Spirit within you and bring it about that you walk in My statutes, and are careful and follow My ordinances. (Ezek. 36:25-27)

We learn from this Scripture that the second birth is all about God's intervention to rebuild us from our sinful nature by giving us a new heart and a new spirit. God also said, "I will put my Spirit within you." It is how to be born again—it is the spiritual transformation and newness of life (of mind and heart) by the action of the Holy Spirit. It is God giving to you His Spirit.

Sad that you cannot have the Holy Spirit's indwelling in your body by your own navigation and maneuvering. No one can be saved through one's invented plans or schemes. The second birth is God-given, and you cannot have it by your own good works. For we are saved by grace through faith and not through our perfect obedience to the Law. (Cf. Eph. 2:8-9)

As mentioned, the born-again experience involves the Holy Spirit's intervention in the soul. It is not the result of your darling self-righteousness.

The Possession of God's Spirit in the Born-Again Experience

The salvation of our soul from God's wrath because of sin is always obtained through the force of the second birth, also known as the born-again experience (or you may call it "the born again phenomenon"). Christ said, to retrace our point, that no one can enter the kingdom of God unless one is **born again**. It is Christ who requires it; we cannot invent another path to heaven.

We want to stress that born again is not Pentecostalism or Baptist or speaking in tongues. It is not a denomination or a particular church practice. Rather, it is about the indwelling of God's Spirit. Here is how the apostle Paul describes it:

> "Or do you not know that your body is a temple of the Holy Spirit who is in you, whom you have from God, and that you are not your own? For you have been bought with a price: therefore glorify God in your body." (1 Cor. 6:19-20)

A born-again person is possessed by God's Spirit, and the world cannot understand him. I tried to gather the common reason behind the exodus of "Christian" leaders away from the faith. My finding is that these fake Christians are so focused on the world. They demand the accommodation of pop culture to grow the church. And what they dislike most is the believers' born-again peculiarity — "because they are not of the world, even as I [Christ] am not of the world"! (John 17:14)

After Joshua Harris left his ministry, he said that the genuine Christians "contributed to a culture of exclusion and bigotry."[5]

Christ was a non-conformist. The fake Christians may have called our Lord a bigot. In Matthew 11:16-17, Christ said: "But

---

[5] Bote, Joshua. He wrote the Christian case against dating. Now he's splitting from his wife and faith. Usatoday.com. https://www.usatoday.com/story/news/nation/2019/07/29/joshua-harris-i-kissed-dating-goodbye-i-am-not-christian/1857934001/ (accessed May 4, 2020).

to what shall I compare this generation? It is like children sitting in the market places, who call out to the other children, and say, 'We played the flute for you, and you did not dance; we sang a dirge, and you did not mourn.'"

The residence of God's Spirit in the soul of the born-again Christian explains the cause of their spiritual attitude, but it is not bigotry. It is the mark of a transformed life as written by the apostle Paul:

> "Don't copy the behavior and customs of this world, but let God transform you into a new person by changing the way you think. Then you will learn to know God's will for you, which is good and pleasing and perfect." (Rom. 12:2, NLT)

The Bible said Christ will intercede (Rom. 8:34) and the Holy Spirit inside our body would grieve when we sinned. (Eph. 4:30) The born-again experience is better understood by the regular involvement of God's Spirit in our lives.

The Spirit's Seal in a Born-Again Experience

Paul said the Holy Spirit is from God. It is given to live in you and make your body the house or temple of God's Spirit. He also added that "you have been bought with a price." Simply put, Christ purchased your salvation by His own blood. If you trust this Gospel or Good News that Jesus Christ died on the cross to pay your own death sentence because of sin and unrighteousness, then our Lord Jesus will send to you the Spirit of God. It is the seal of His ownership of you as His child. Paul taught it in Ephesians 1:13:

> "In Him, you also, after listening to the message of truth, the gospel of your salvation—having also believed, you were **sealed** in Him with the Holy Spirit of promise."

Before my conversion, I opposed the Evangelicals' teaching

that without spiritual rebirth, we are not children of God. Now I realized that if God really owns me, He must have a mark of ownership in my soul. (Cf. John 6:27) Without this signature, I am unsaved and a stranger in heaven. Without Christ in my heart, I don't have a God in this life. (Cf. Eph. 2:12)

The Bible has always a supply for truth. Do we need God's imprint on our souls? Here is Paul's teaching: "Now He who establishes us with you in Christ and anointed us is God, who also sealed us and gave us the Spirit in our hearts as a pledge." (2 Cor. 1:21-22) The God of the Holy Scriptures, the Father of Christ, has the seal of His ownership, who is God's Spirit in us—given to us as a pledge or guarantee!

The carnal soul does not have any of these promises. Christ even made it worse, when He said that the non-born-again life is separated from God (Cf. Is. 59:2) and therefore, fathered by the devil. To those who claimed Abraham was their father, Christ said, "You are of your father the devil, and you want to do the desires of your father. He was a murderer from the beginning, and does not stand in the truth because there is no truth in him. Whenever he speaks a lie, he speaks from his own nature, for he is a liar and the father of lies." (John 8:44)

Who are these devil-fathered people? Well, all those who reject Jesus, for He said, "If God were your Father, you would love Me, for I proceeded forth and have come from God." (John 8:42)

Instead of a divine seal and pledge of ownership, Christ disowns those who are not born-again Christians, including those pretenders and sympathizers, who are active in different Christian ministries.

Harris left the Lord's church because he does not have the born-again experience we noticed from the genuine children of God.

The sealing off of the Holy Spirit on your soul is the process where the born-again life gets its birth. And the Scripture mentioned above (in Ephesians 1:13) requires two things. The first is the "listening to the message of truth, the gospel of your salvation"; the second is "having also believed." These are the requisites to be born again. Where is your good works or generosity or ego in this divine plan to clothe you with the promised immortality by the second birth? Well, God did not call on your "good side" because He knew you don't have one. In Romans 6:23, Paul said, "[F]or all have sinned and fall short of the glory of God." It is the third requirement, may I add, to be born of God's Spirit—we must have the firm conviction that we are sinners before God and helpless to get the second birth by our own means!

Listen and Believe to Have a Born-Again Experience

In sum, to be born again we need to accept the truth that we are full-blown transgressors of the law and unworthy to live forever. "There is none righteous, no, not one." (Rom. 3:10, KJV) Therefore, our salvation is God-given; it is accessed by God's grace or undeserved favor. "For by grace you have been saved." (Eph. 2:8a) As such, we need to listen "to the message of truth, the gospel of your salvation" and to believe ("having also believed." — Cf. Eph. 1:13) the Good News.

How to LISTEN to the message of truth and how to BELIEVE it? When Christ taught Nicodemus how to be born again, the latter listened and asked, "How can a man be born when he is old? He cannot enter a second time into his mother's womb and be born, can he?" (John 3:4) I don't have a better conclusion than that Nicodemus LISTENED; he even took part in the discussion and even asked a truly relevant question. Again, this happened because he listened to Jesus.

Look what took place after Christ's death? Nicodemus joined with Joseph of Arimathea in burying Jesus:

> "Nicodemus, who had first come to Him by night, also came, bringing a mixture of myrrh and aloes, about a hundred pounds weight." (John 19:39)

How do you see it? Obvious. Nicodemus believed in Christ and in His Word. Ephesians 1:13 draws a perfect application with Nicodemus. He listened and believed. He got the second birth through the sealing off of his soul with the Holy Spirit after listening and believing.

How about you? Are you a born-again Christian? If so, you will live forever in heaven with Jesus. For he "who believes in the Son has eternal life; but he who does not obey the Son will not see life, but the wrath of God abides on him." (John 3:36)

As an inquirer of unbelief, I always take a hike at the Scripture in Luke 16:31 which explains the root of people's rejection of the truth (not listening; not believing). Christ said in His parable of the Rich Man and Lazarus that, "If they do not listen to Moses and the Prophets, they will not be persuaded even if someone rises from the dead." Believe the Bible (which Christ referred to as "Moses and the Prophets") as the very Word of God if you want to listen and believe in Christ and become sealed with the Holy Spirit. Listen and believe like Nicodemus—there is no other way to become born again and live with Christ in heaven forever!

4. PSEUDO-CHRISTIAN DISTINCTIVES

"Not everyone who says to Me, 'Lord, Lord,' will enter the kingdom of heaven." — Matthew 7:21.

The Pseudo-Christian Has a False Conversion

THE FAKE CHRISTIAN does not have the second birth experience. Hence, when he says "Amen" or "Praise the Lord," he utters it from practice and out of habit, and not out of love for Christ and His Word. The unsaved person can do all things done in the Christian Church like submission to water baptism, worship-service attendance, preaching, etc. except that he does not have the living hope of eternal life in his soul. In the Charismatic services, he would jump and dance and give touching testimonies, complete with adjectives and drama—but they are just a play of words outside of a firm conviction that when death comes, Christ would be there to lift him.

I met a man (the son of a pastor) who got a top position in his company. A church guy from early childhood, he never missed a Sunday in the fellowship. But he was not a born-again (although he thought he was) Christian. He had an affair with his secretary, and everybody knew it. One day, he attended a worship service in another church, and there got saved. How did it happen? From his testimony, he experienced for the first time in his life the power of God's Word when used by the Holy Spirit. He realized how sinful he was before God, and his desire for Christ's forgiveness blew hard into his soul. He saw daylight on how he lived for three decades without a working relationship with Jesus, our Lord. The second birth is an encounter with God and those who don't experience it ridicule all who lay claim of its truth. True, the attitude of darkness against the light will never change.

The Pseudo-Christian Doesn't Believe in Prayer

It is easy to spot a nominal Christian in the church. He is a pastor-dependent even in prayers. In his emergencies, he would ask his pastor to pray for him as if he couldn't reach Jesus without the intercession of his elder. As an old man, I have health issues and I always asked my wife to pray for, and with me. Even the apostle Paul asked for prayers. But the fake Christian does not know Jesus; he doesn't have faith in the efficacy of his own prayers!

From back in the day, I had a church member who dumped upon me his prayer requests during the wee hours of the morning (in his house). After around four years, I met him again and learned he had a recent wife. He left his first wife as he promised he would after finding a job. (He was jobless for a long time.) He is the model of a man who is not born again.

When sick or having a trial, the nominal Christians value the prayers of their friends, pastor, and fellow church members more than their own.

The Pseudo-Christian Has No Stable Faith

The faith of the pseudo-Christians does not have deep roots from the Holy Scriptures. They worship Jesus without spontaneity, only plain conformity of the herd mindset. They don't have God in this life, only religion. When the non-Christian, the Christ-rejecting cultic person would approach them, they wouldn't know the spiritual harm as a result of the fellowship, because the Holy Spirit does not indwell them. The Christian privilege to discern spiritual things won't work with them.

John said: "If anyone comes to you and does not bring this teaching, do not receive him into your house, and do not give him a greeting." (2 John 1:10) The Jehovah's Witness, for example, denies Christ, but the counterfeit Christian does not understand the Bible requirement to turn down the cults.

The genuine Christian would share the Gospel with all unsaved ones, but the nominal Christians cannot share Christ whom they don't have.

The unregenerated soul does not worship God alone, because what he wants is a group event with the pastor leading the activity. In his solitude, the nominal Christian doesn't have a God to call his own.

When there is an organizational meeting or other worldly events in the Christian assembly, the unregenerate wants to shine more like the floods of the natural people desiring acceptance. He loves a position in the church organization.

Ask him about God, he would share with you what he learned from Sunday schools, except the things in his heart because there is no God inside him. Unbelief, including the pretensions of faith, is just as complex as genuine Christianity itself.

The ostensible Christian loves fanaticism and superstitions, too. He sees the pastor as a little god and the church as his savior in the ebb and flow of life. In fairness, he's a giver. His main doctrine is to please God by his efforts, like pleasing his Mom by washing dishes.

If he cannot get material help from his church of membership, he would transfer to another assembly. He would use the names of prominent Christians with his first group to achieve his goal of becoming a deacon. This story is endless of deacons and towering leaders in the churches who are not born again.

The Pseudo-Christian Has No Real Love for the Word of God

As a born-again Christian for around 40 years now, I noticed the babes in Christ, most of them unsaved, not bringing a Bible (before the age of the smartphone) during Sunday services. It is a reality check: the fake Christians don't read the Holy Scriptures. If they would study the Scriptures, it wouldn't be connected to their thirst for the truth, but prideful discussions and intellectualism. Paul said they are "always learning and never able to come to the knowledge of the truth." (2 Tim. 3:7)

What is important to them is church fellowship, whatever the doctrines. Their interest in a sermon is health and prosperity topics—those that don't challenge the conscience and the spiritual realities about sin and hell. They received baptism solely for membership qualifications. They seem to know all about Christianity (baptism, the Lord's Table, fellowships) except our Lord Jesus Christ.

This teaching from the lips of Christ suits them: "You search the Scriptures because you think that in them you have eternal life; it is these that testify about Me; and you are unwilling to come to Me so that you may have life." (John 5:39-40)

The false Christians have all the adjectives about Christianity but know nothing about Christ our Lord. They are susceptible to the Charismatics' blind emotionalism. They are the most active church members who don't have the assurance of eternal salvation.

The unsaved "Christians" love man-made teachings, those that tickled their ears. "For the time will come," wrote the apostle Paul, "when they will not endure sound doctrine; but wanting to have their ears tickled, they will accumulate for themselves teachers in accordance to their own desires." (2 Tim. 4:3)

The Pseudo-Christian Has No Hope of Eternal Life

I shared a story about our church member a long time ago who gave birth shouting Christ's name. When the pain got more excruciating, she shouted her mother's name instead. The genuine Christian puts his hope on Christ alone. John said, "These things I have written to you who believe in the name of the Son of God, so that you may know that you have eternal life." (1 John 5:13) We have hope in Christ, and not just in this life, but the hope of eternal salvation from God's wrath.

The counterfeit Christian does not put his trust in Jesus. Hence, the Holy Spirit cannot live in his soul to give him hope. Wrote the apostle Paul that since you listened to and believed the truth, the gospel of your salvation, God sealed you with the Holy Spirit of promise—as a pledge of our inheritance—as proof that God redeemed and possessed us. (Cf. Eph. 1:13-14) The fake Christians just don't have the seal of the Holy Spirit for God's ownership of our souls. No biblical hope will ever thrive in the heart devoid of God's eternal Spirit. It is worth repeating the gravity of Christ's requirement for us to experience the second birth through the indwelling of the Holy Spirit.

We need to be born again by the spirit of God.

The Pseudo-Christian Opposes the Genuine Christians

Wrote the apostle Paul: "For the flesh sets its desire against the Spirit, and the Spirit against the flesh; for these are in opposition to one another." (Gal. 5:27) Note that one cause of chaos in the family is when a Christian marries an unbeliever.

The spiritual soul opposes the carnal one—vice versa. It also happens in the church, more so when the fake Christians control most of the membership. We read reports from the U.S. about Christian churches splitting over gay marriage. It is the point. The pseudo-Christians hate our fundamentalism; they will soon populate the Laodicean churches throughout the world.

I attended a church meeting where a rich old woman stood up and imposed her carnal and unscriptural ideas in the church. Later, I learned the church split because of her.

The ostensible Christians can pray cool prayers like a torrent of words, to use Spurgeon's observation. But they don't have the fruit of the Spirit, as discussed by Paul in Galatians. Why, because they are not born again.

Without the second birth event in life, which is synonymous with divine forgiveness and the eternal salvation of the soul, the make-believe Christian could only find religion in Christianity, never a loving relationship with the resurrected Son of God and Redeemer. The pseudo-Christians could just be outsiders if we were to resemble born-again Christianity to an enormous box. But truth be told, Christ is waiting for them to come in by receiving and trusting our Lord and Savior Jesus based on the solid grounding from the Word of God.

5. OF NOMINAL CHRISTIANITY

*He who believes in Him is not judged; he who
does not believe has been judged already, because
he has not believed in the name of the only
begotten Son of God. — John 3:18.*

THE NOMINAL CHRISTIANS are those Christians in name only. They are not a part of the born-again followers of Jesus. Let's talk about their confusion from distinct vantage points.

Nominal Christianity: Its Intrinsic Fanaticism

In Matthew 7, Christ taught about the second birth teaching from a fresh angle. He noticed that the false Christians are also calling Him Lord. (v. 21) In short, they are also praying. What is crucial in this Scripture is Christ's "I never knew you" declaration on those who cast out demons and perform miracles in His name.

It is the profile of unbelief. The fake Christians would love to put God into an embarrassing situation. One Charismatic group, for example, held a healing session, but after half an hour of casting out the demons in the name of Jesus, the patient's convulsion persisted. Then their leader shouted, "Satan, get out of him, let's fight one on one!"

The answered prayers of the born-again Christians have mesmerized the fake ones. Pharaoh ordered Moses' miracles duplicated. But "The Lord knows those who are His." (2 Tim. 2:19) To those who are not born of God, "the Lord would not listen to your voice nor give ear to you." (Deut. 1:45b) Superstition and the invention of "old wives fables" for a church doctrine capture those missing Christ's Spirit in their souls. The nominal Christians' empty and unanswered prayers work against them. Fanaticism becomes the side effect after experiencing Christ's rejection of their cries.

Fanaticism means a religious devotion without evidence. And from this definition, we find tons of religious beliefs under this category. The Bible does not teach superstition and religious madness. What it teaches is Christ's glorification in whatever we do. "Whatever you do in word or deed," wrote the apostle Paul, "do everything in the name of the Lord Jesus, giving thanks through Him to God the Father." (Colossians 3 and verse 17.)

One fanatical practice is bibliolatry or the worship of a book, the Bible. Born-again Christianity does not endorse such an unsound reverence. I heard one nominal Christian say that to find God's will, he would open his Bible with his eyes closed, and drop his forefinger on the page. The verse it touches is the will of God for him. This is fanaticism in the Siberia of scriptural ignorance. This is bibliolatry or the practice of deifying the Bible and idolizing it to the level of a god. But Christ does not teach it!

I met an old schoolteacher one day who told me her conversion started by accidentally opening Exodus 20 where she found a verse against worshipping idols—against Catholicism! (Cf. Ex. 20:3-4) This instance is not Bibliolatry, for this woman was not yet a believer and did not even own a Bible at this time.

After attending the preaching of Saint Ambrose, the Bishop of Milan, in around 386 A.D., Saint Augustine heard a group of children singing, "Pick it up and read it. Pick it up and read it." It marked the beginning of Saint Augustine's conversion story. He opened and read the book of Romans and found these two powerful verses for him: "Let's behave properly as in the day, not in carousing and drunkenness, not in sexual promiscuity and debauchery, not in strife and jealousy. But put on the Lord Jesus Christ, and make no provision for the flesh in regard to its lusts." (Rom. 13:13-14) But such was not a Bible worship either. The case was different. I think these two experiences just mentioned fall under Hebrews 4:12, where the Word of God is sharper than any two-edged sword when used by the Holy Spirit.

Two of my church members before (both were former Pentecostals!), for another illustration, told me not to pray over the daughter of one of them, since they had prayed and declared already with God their petition for the girl to pass the bar exams. In our casual conversations, they always told me they put confidence with the word "declare," as if God must answer them with it. Long story short, they declared or prayed for the girl's exams twice and she failed twice. It's always a bad idea to rely on fanatical and man-made doctrines.

Why is fanaticism indispensable with nominal Christianity? Well, it's just as natural as the dog barking or cat meowing. Superstition and fanaticism always pull strings on all false religions. The veneration of the dead, for example, is part of Catholicism. As such, it leads the Catholics to pray for the souls in purgatory and give money to the church for the soul's release. It is fanaticism since the Bible does not teach it. The savior of our souls is Christ, not the Catholic Church.

One Pentecostal pastor, for another example, preached that the Lord would be in their midst the following Sunday, and the sign would be the scent of a perfume. During the next worship service, the pastor shook his members' hands, and all of them smelled the sweet fragrance of something like *Eau de Parfum*. And the congregants believed the trick! The Lord they waited for was the pastor himself. Just a pathetic deception, but the nominal Christians are madly in love with signs and wonders. For them, it's better to be blind followers than to know the truth. Fanaticism is the devil's blindfold, and salvation from this demonic control happens only by genuine faith in Christ and His Word.

Paul said, Satan exerts "all the deception of wickedness for those who perish, because they did not receive the love of the truth so as to be saved." (2 Thess. 2:10)

In the biblical eye, the nominal Christians are just like the Muslims or Hindus in their level of unbelief and ridicule of our Lord Jesus.

Nominal Christianity: Its Doctrinal Turbulence

After songwriter Marty Sampson of the "Hillsong United," left Christianity, he wrote that, "Christians can be the most judgmental people on the planet — they can also be some of the most beautiful and loving people. But it's not for me."[6]

It is happening since day one of the Christian faith. Aside from Judas' betrayal of Christ, Paul's companions left him. Note 2 Timothy 4:16: "At my first defense no one supported me, but all deserted me; may it not be counted against them." And the bottom line why are "Christians" leaving Christianity is the absence of the second birth experience.

Have you heard of someone accusing you of practicing "toxic Christianity?"

Here is higher-dose toxicity. The televangelist, Jim Bakker, who helped in popularizing Pat Robertson's "The 700 Club," divorced his wife, got imprisoned for fraud—after authoring over a dozen books and enjoying the label as an expert in Revelation! Wiki described him as "an American televangelist,

---

[6] French, David. Another Pop-Culture Christian Loses His Faith. Nationalreview.com.
https://www.nationalreview.com/2019/08/another-pop-culture-christian-loses-his-faith/ (accessed October 3, 2020)

entrepreneur, and convicted fraudster."[7]

"'[Obama's] reign,' Bakker prayed in November 2016, let him 'change the rules of America, to change even the Bible's standards.'"[8]

Those born of God don't teach to let Obama change the Bible's standards. Bakker, Sampson, like Jimmy Swaggart, came from the same denomination.

The Charismatic groups are the primary target audience of Christ in Matthew 7 since He said: "I never knew you" to those "miracle workers" mentioned in His teaching.

Whatever your denominational affiliation, if you've confidence in your shallow doctrines, it is because you don't have an authentic Christianity.

A former Pentecostal man for 50 years, for example, wrote his observation about the movement:

"But after all of this, it wasn't God that we saw, it was man. From Toronto, to Brownsville, to Cottage Hill, and many more places I could name, there were no miracles, no power, no gifts, no healings, nothing but the theatrical antics and delusions of men. What was claimed for the great power of God was nothing more than musical hype and psychologically induced emotionalism."[9]

Want to know more about shallow doctrines? They are

[7] https://en.wikipedia.org/wiki/Jim_Bakker

[8] McKinney, Kelsey. The Second Coming Of Televangelist Jim Bakker. buzzfeednews.com. https://www.buzzfeednews.com/article/kelseymckinney/second-coming-of-televangelist-jim-bakker (accessed May 3, 2020).

[9] Davis, William Charles, Jr. Why I am no longer a Pentecostal. Oldpaths.com. http://www.oldpaths.com/Archive/Davis/William/Charles/Jr/1952/Pentecostalism.html (accessed November 27, 2020)

"theatrical antics and delusions of men"; they are "musical hype and psychologically induced emotionalism." Well, that's the dark side of extreme Pentecostalism. This denomination, in fairness, has won more souls to Christ, according to the Pentecostal websites, than the older groups. And for a fairer evaluation, Pentecostalism and the entire Charismatic Movement are also responsible for raising more Christian fanatics, which even their writers and most popular preachers agree and give caution.

What about the doctrinal turbulence among the non-Pentecostals?

In my other works, I wrote about one "pastor who said that God's Word is like a pistol: it releases the 'bullet,' even if it is fired accidentally by someone ignorant about firing a pistol. In a word that pastor said God's Word gives off power once shared even if exhorted by the unbeliever."[10]

Tozer calls this teaching "textualism." Do you want to sleep? Listen to a preacher who believes in the power of the Bible without understanding the anointing of the Holy Spirit. It illustrates a shallow doctrine, where the preacher gives all his might to preach the Word without the unction of the Holy Spirit.

I heard many preachers saying we are indwelt and sealed with the Holy Spirit, and therefore, the Holy Spirit is always present, illuminating the Word when we share the Gospel. It's just like a pistol fired by a kid. The bullet just explodes. This unsound teaching is one reason for the Laodicean atmosphere in most Baptist churches. The result is the increase of nominal Christianity among the Baptists!

But after Jesus breathed the Holy Spirit on His disciples,

---

[10] Espina, Jun P. "CHRISTIAN TEACHINGS REVISITED: 32 Christ-Uplifting Chapters for Both the Truth Seekers and the Skeptics", p. 60.

and said, "Receive the Holy Spirit" (John 20:22), He also said in Luke 24:49, don't preach yet. Your fire-a-pistol doctrine won't work. Wait for the infilling of the Holy Spirit for service. Observe Christ's instruction: "And behold, I am sending forth the promise of My Father upon you; but you are to stay in the city until you are clothed with power from on high."

Don't preach yet, guys. Stay at Jerusalem, "until you are clothed with power from on high," until you are filled with the Holy Spirit, and your preaching would not induce the congregants to sleep.

We all know Dwight Moody, and here is how he expound the teaching about the infilling of the Holy Spirit from his sermon titled, ENDUEMENT FOR SERVICE:

I SUPPOSE if I could put the question and ask those who are filled with the Spirit to respond, very few if any would be heard from. And yet we read in Ephesians 5:18 that this is a command: "Be ye filled with the Spirit." God commands us to be filled with the Spirit; and if we are not filled, it is because we are living beneath our privileges. I think that is the great trouble with Christendom today: we are not living up on the plane where God would have us live. In the 20th chapter of John's Gospel, and the 22nd verse, are these words: "And when He had said this, He breathed on them, and said unto them, Receive ye the Holy Ghost." Now, those men had already the Holy Ghost dwelling in them. They would never have left their fishing smacks and followed Christ during those three years of humiliation and suffering if it hadn't been for the Spirit of God working in them. But almost the first thing after the resurrection, when our Lord appeared to His disciples and showed them His pierced hands and His wounded side, He breathed upon them and said: "Receive ye the Holy Ghost." Yet again, after that, as we see in Luke 24:49, He said: "Behold, I send the promise of My Father upon you:

but tarry ye in the city of Jerusalem, until ye be endued with power from on high." If those men needed to be endued with power, do you think we are going to be used without it? The great trouble with many of us is, that we are working for God without power. We are sons of God - no doubt about that - and daughters of God. We can "read our titles clear to mansions in the skies," but we are sons and daughters without power. That is the trouble."[11]

The Pentecostals' insistence on the power of the Holy Spirit, which leads somehow to fanaticism, has pushed most Baptists to the corner and skip the prevailing issues about the Holy Spirit's presence and power in our midst instead of studying them. It's like saying, "the Pentecostal's Holy Spirit teaching is fanatical, so I would not waste time exploring from the Scriptures about the Holy Spirit. I don't want to understand the biblical baptism of the Holy Spirit—it's just so pentecostalized!"

In his book titled "Real Worship," Warren Wiersbe said, "I must admit that I tend to agree with Bishop Handley Moule who said that he would rather tone down a fanatic than resurrect a corpse. It would be better not to have either extreme, of course; but if I have to make a choice, give me the fanatic."[12]

I commented on Wiersbe's "Real Worship" in my book, "Christian Teachings Revisited," as I cannot agree with his

---

[11] Moody, D. L. Enduement for Service. 1timothy4-13.com. https://www.1timothy4-13.com/files/teach/enduement.html (accessed November 27, 2020).

[12] Warren W. Wiersbe, Real Worship (Tennessee: Oliver-Nelson Books, 1986), p. 24.

adding so much Pentecostal flavor to his work. But when he said give me the fanatic, I thought he had a point! The older denominations have lost their appeal as the authentic ambassadors for Christ because of too much doctrinal preciseness, and too little grasp for the fullness of the Holy Spirit for soul-winning power.

There is doctrinal turbulence on all sides of the varying Christian persuasions, and the most distressed among them are the people-centered, miracle-assisted, and income-focused megachurches and their respective satellite groups. They are the most addicted to their "musical hype and psychologically induced emotionalism," and the most vulnerable to the unscriptural doctrines of nominal Christianity.

Nominal Christianity: The Chaos of Its Practices

Today, almost all charismatic churches have sessions on demon casting and miracles. While most fundamentalists like the fake Baptists flounder on their Laodicean paralysis, the unsaved Pentecostals, on the other hand, enjoy their addiction to signs and wonders.

The saddest thing in the chaos of the nominal Christians is their expectation to enter God's kingdom because of what they did for Christ. But our Lord won't allow them, for He will honor His rule to accept only those born of the Spirit of God. "[U]nless you are born again, you cannot see the Kingdom of God." (John 3:3b, NLT)

In Matthew 7, our Lord taught that His born-again followers did the will of the Father (v. 21), while the false Christians did not. But what is this will of the Father? Christ told Nicodemus in John 3:16 that "whoever believes in Him shall not perish, but have eternal life." That is the Father's will—to trust our eternal future to Jesus. The thief on the cross did it before he landed in Paradise. Here is John 6:40 for the well-defined translation of this teaching: "For this is the will of My Father, that everyone who beholds the Son and believes in Him will have eternal life, and I Myself will raise him up on the last day."

The nominal Christians practice man-made doctrines, but our Lord disapproves of extra-biblical slants. "Their worship is a farce," taught Christ, "for they teach man-made ideas as commands from God." (Mark 7:7, NLT)

Someone wrote about "the world of tongues, visions, prophecies, ecstasies, dancing, falling down slain" as the false teachings of the Charismatic groups. The devil infiltrates Bible Christianity (Baptist, Evangelicals, et al.) by his deceptive teachings and practices.

It is not exclusive to the "emotionalized" denominations.

The non-Pentecostal groups have their own chaos in their practices. One is the urge to humanize the Gospel like preaching sin as if God can tolerate it, or hell as if it is not hot as a lake of fire and brimstone.

Just like the rest of the Christian denominations, the non-charismatic groups have their issues with unwanted pregnancies, single mothers, divorce, drug addiction, and homosexuality. The ordination of female pastors caps the chaos in the practices of the nominal Christians.

We don't teach that born-again Christians are immune from all the evils that have blackened Christianity as a faith system.

Some girls who were truly born of God have also suffered from the humiliation of teen pregnancy or drug addiction. The men, likewise, got into tons of unchristian practices.

It is in our teaching, however, that no matter the trials, a born-again Christian will always win in this world since the

Scripture teaches that if God is with us, who is against us? Here is how Paul taught it: "What then shall we say to these things? If God is for us, who is against us? He who did not spare His own Son, but delivered Him over for us all, how will He not also with Him freely give us all things?" (Rom. 8:32-33)

God will give us freely all things in Jesus, until our Christianity is tested untrue, and not the born-again Christianity we throw light upon in this paper.

Nominal Christianity: The Character of Its Faith

From this Scripture in John 6:40, we find the clear-cut difference between the false and the genuine Christians. The counterfeits assume the devil's faith in Christ, while the true Christians behold the Son crucified and believe in Him and the Gospel that Jesus died for our sins and rose from the grave. This is the character of faith that saves. Hence, it would cause Christ to fill their souls with His Spirit! "For this is the will of My Father, that everyone who BEHOLDS the Son and BELIEVES in Him will have eternal life." (Note that a born-again person is a born-of-the-Spirit individual.)

Abraham is the father of faith. He waited for God's promised son to him even when Sarah, his wife, has long past childbearing. (Gen. 18:11) The essence of this Abrahamic faith is complete trust in the Word of God. Paul ratified the doctrine by saying that "faith comes from hearing, and hearing by the word of Christ." I attended a birthday party of an active church leader who cooked 60 eggs for having reached age 60. Where did he hear it? The Bible did not say, "Hearing by the word of your unbelieving mother," but by the word of Christ (NASB).

I met various forms of unbelief in the church, and the heart-rending of it all is that the fake Christians do not know they are unsaved sinners before God. One church member, for example, testified that he loved the Baptist church because her members visited him while he was struggling to survive his heart surgery. We don't have a problem with that. Appreciation is a positive attitude builder. But we cannot be saved because of our knowledge of the Lord's church, but our knowing Jesus. I also met someone who said he loved the food and fellowship in the church; his giving cash during a Sunday worship is just returned to him in the form of a church's fellowship lunch. Have you heard of a husband who attended church to please his wife? It's common. The rise of fake Christians cannot be denied, but most leaders tolerate them for their contribution in the offering box.

We can classify the quality of faith as the nominal Christian professes, and sad that it is about everything unscriptural.

The fake Christian's faith can be described as faith in Christ plus something. He believes in Christ, but also believes in his own righteousness. It's always a fifty-fifty relationship. "Lord, this is your part, and this is mine."

In salvation, he believes in faith in Christ plus baptism, the giving of offerings, or speaking in tongues, or all three.

His Christianity formula is as unmistakable as Christ plus something, plus the Church or the priest to get closer to God, or Christ plus his good deeds to have salvation and eternal life.

Do we believe in good works, too, as born-again Christians? Yes, we do. But we see our self-righteousness as the result of our faith, not the cause or root of our friendly and acceptable relationship with God.

We cannot tell God to look at us with favor since we give money to the poor or the church. The favorite verse of Henry Sy, Jr., the son of the Philippines' richest man, is found in 1 Samuel 12:24. It says: "Only fear the Lord and serve Him in truth with all your heart; for consider what great things He has done for you." Our life is God's indefinable gift to us, and our salvation through Christ, our most unspeakable privilege. Our good deeds, whatever they are, cannot outshine God's goodness and generosity toward us.

Henry Sy, Jr. and his siblings own 76 "SM Supermalls" in the Philippines as of December 2020 and 25 more malls are to be opened to reach 101 superstores. They have also seven malls in China.[13] Sy probably reflected on his immense wealth as the great things God has done for their family.

For us who don't have reached any material success in life, we can say that the greatest thing God has done for us is His giving to us Jesus. Our Lord ransomed us from our slavery to sin and gave us forgiveness, salvation, and eternal life through His own blood. We would live forever in heaven if we would believe and give our trust in Him as our only Savior and Lord. "For God so loved the world, that He gave His only begotten Son, that whoever believes in Him shall not perish, but have eternal life."

Sad that everything we believe concerning Christ, the nominal Christian would also give his assent without understanding why.

In the Parable of the Sower, Christ taught that if you don't understand, you cannot bear fruit. Observe Matthew 11:23:

"And the one on whom seed was sown on the good soil, this is the man who hears the word and understands it; who indeed bears fruit and brings forth, some a hundredfold, some sixty, and some thirty."

What's the point? Well, the born-again Christian

---

[13] SM Supermalls. En.wikipedia.org. https://en.wikipedia.org/wiki/SM_Supermalls (accessed January 18, 2021)

understands what he believes in. But the nominal Christian believes in things he does not care about. It is the character of his faith. He is not a truth seeker!

Nominal Christianity: The Spiritual Nature of Its Deception

The ugliest divine judgment the pseudo-Christians will face in this life is God's helping them to believe what is false. God won't lower His standards. If you would not believe, He would help cement your unbelief. It is how God works. In Isaiah 66:2, God looks to "him who is humble and contrite of spirit, and who trembles at My word." In Romans chapter one, the apostle Paul wrote that God gave the unbelievers "over to a depraved mind." Jesus used to leave the crowd and go to a solitary place to pray instead of brainwashing the people and feeding them with all available biblical reasons to believe in Him.

We need to draw near to God and seek His face. Jesus did not do many miracles in His hometown because of their unbelief. (Matt. 13:58) Paul wrote that if you do not love the truth—the fake Christians' typical attitude—then God "will send upon them a deluding influence so that they will believe what is false, in order that they all may be judged who did not believe the truth, but took pleasure in wickedness." (2 Thess. 2:11-12) In Christ's parable of the Rich Man and Lazarus, Abraham lectured that, "If they do not listen to Moses and the Prophets [meaning faith in the Holy Bible], they will not be persuaded even if someone [Jesus Christ] rises from the dead." While the genuine Christians love the truth, the fake believers favor falsehood and even support those who practice them and give them a "hearty approval." (See Rom. 1:32)

Pretension is awful, for God Himself will increase the unbelief of those rejecting Jesus after listening to the word of truth, the Gospel.

Speaking of your faith in Christ, God pays attention to your heart and helps you see the fogs in your eyes toward our Savior. Thomas the Apostle rejected Christ's resurrection until he could see by his naked eye and touch the hand of the risen Jesus. Do we see the spiritual nature of Thomas's unbelief? Well, he disbelieved Jesus (and His Word!), who resurrected from the grave. And that unbelief had a spiritual attachment and reality. Any rejection of Christ involves the spiritual realm because Christ is the Truth and the Lord of all.

Wrote Paul that God "raised Him from the dead and seated Him at His right hand in the heavenly places, far above all rule and authority and power and dominion, and every name that is named, not only in this age but also in the one to come. And He put all things in subjection under His feet." (Eph. 1:20b-22a)

The nominal Christians' pretension of faith is a concern in God's sight because He is a hater of sin, and one's rejection of Jesus is a severe transgression based on Christ's teaching that God's wrath will abide on all unbelievers.

Nominal Christianity is fake Christianity. People won't be saved through this persuasion. Satan deceived all the followers of this group, and that makes their deception transmits a spiritual badge.

Nominal Christianity: Understanding Its Salvation Teaching

We have filled the pages of this work with the biblical teaching that our scriptural salvation from God's judgment is secured exclusively from the finished work of Christ at Calvary. "For by grace you have been saved through faith; and that not of yourselves, it is the gift of God; not as a result of works, so that no one may boast. Knowing that you were not redeemed with perishable things like silver or gold from your futile way of life inherited from your forefathers, but with precious blood, as of a lamb unblemished and spotless, the blood of Christ." (Eph. 2:8-9; 1 Pet. 1:18-19)

The nominal or false Christian does not encounter biblical salvation, which we also describe as the born-again experience. As such, he does not have the scriptural doctrine about salvation in his heart.

Christ's disciple, Thomas, was a typical nominal Christian. When Christ resurrected Lazarus from the grave, he was there. He saw what was impossible. When Mary Magdalene got born again, he noticed it. Yet, he didn't know how to become a genuine believer despite all of Christ's teachings and miracles he heard and witnessed.

Today, all nominal believers of Christ do not know they are unsaved, and that Christ rejects them. Can you imagine Thomas' unbelief after the resurrection testimonies of Magdalene, John, Peter, and the two men journeying toward Emmaus? If you are a doubter like Thomas, today is your chance to experience the second birth and enjoy Christ's Spirit's presence in your soul.

Believe and receive Jesus in your heart. Pray to Him this minute and invite Him to save and forgive you. Experience freedom from Satan's blindfold and deception. Do it, and meet Christ's Spirit in your soul!

I did the same thing and it worked for me, and my proof is this book. I couldn't have written this paper without familiarity with the born-again experience.

The crucified two thieves were with Christ representing the two faiths in the world, which is faith in Christ or rejection of Him. The good news is that you are still alive and can still believe in Jesus' blood shed on the cross to ransom your sinful soul. It is the only way to get a second birth and live forever through such faith.

According to tradition, Thomas the Apostle went to India and got martyred there after 20 years of witnessing for Jesus. But what's in the Bible record heightens our remembrance of Thomas more, for it authenticated the truth on how to get salvation after years of nominal Christianity. After seeing the resurrected Jesus, Thomas declared that Christ was his Lord and God. (John 20:28) But Christ's reply to Thomas has drilled into my heart more, aside from the latter's declaration of my Savior's deity. For Christ said: "Because you have seen Me, have you now believed? Blessed are they who did not see, and yet believed." I am more blessed than Thomas because I believed even without touching the warm hands of the risen Jesus. You can do it, too!

6. WHAT BORN AGAIN IS NOT?

"For he is not a Jew who is one outwardly, nor is circumcision that which is outward in the flesh." — Romans 2:28.

CHRIST HIMSELF TAUGHT the born-again injunction. We need the second birth experience to live in heaven forever. God condensed the absolute divine plan for our salvation from hell judgment in two words, which is **born again**. But, like other biblical teachings, the devil mangled the second birth requirement to enter God's kingdom to suit his deception agenda.

Let's examine in this chapter what born again is not.

First, Born Again is Not a Denomination

The word BAC or Born-Again Christian clutters social media walls as people convey their ridicule or hate on those experiencing the second birth. The Charismatic Christians, for example, love to push the teaching as the ultimate cause of their other extra-biblical dogmas like signs and wonders. "We are born again and advanced Christians," they claimed, and we heard it often! Hence, BAC associates with Pentecostalism for unguarded minds. But it is not true. A genuine Christian is a born-again Christian irrespective of denominational affiliation.

Your church or denomination cannot save you as it cannot produce in you the second birth experience. The Catholic Church's teaching as the keeper or releaser of souls from purgatory is not biblical. Remember also that if you dance or speak in tongues during a worship service because it is your church's doctrine, such a church practice has nothing to do with the second birth. Christ did not tell Nicodemus to do that.

Christian cults (cult means a mirror image of what Christianity is—but not the real thing!) have common symptoms, and one is the teaching that their movement saves a soul or at least assures one of a happy ending. The Jehovah's Witness, for example, teaches that the soul will cease to exist after death. After Armageddon, however, God will allegedly duplicate his soul for the resurrection, and he will inherit the earth (not heaven!) forever.[14] The cults use the same Bible but alter its teachings and revise the language in some passages to suit their doctrines through creating their own Bible translation. The Jehovah's Witness's Bible translation, for instance, edited John 1:1 to show and thus make their members happy that Christ is a little God.[15]

Born again means our soul's salvation from hell because of sin, and no church or denomination can ever give that salvation or eternal life to anyone.

I wrote somewhere about my experience. I left my first denomination since it teaches it's the only genuine church of Jesus and its pastors, the only authentic baptizers. It's an instance of a denomination claiming a share in the born again event. Given this twisted teaching, its leaders assert the born-again experience as something taking place only through the auspices of their church. This doctrine is a fabrication and therefore requiring a merciless rejection.

Mere humans or a group of individuals composing a denomination cannot produce the born again phenomenon.

---

[14] Barker, Jason. "Jehovah's Witnesses and the Immortal Soul". Watchman.org. https://www.watchman.org/articles/jehovahs-witnesses/jehovahs-witnesses-and-the-immortal-soul/ (accessed November 10, 2020).

[15] CARM. "Using the New World Translation to refute the New World Translation: John 1:1." Carm.org. https://carm.org/jehovahs-witnesses/using-the-new-world-translation-john-1-1 (accessed December 5, 2020)

Our Father God used the apostle Peter to convert 3000 souls, just as He used Spurgeon, D. L. Moody, or Billy Graham to lead millions of converted souls. In John 12:26, Christ taught that "If anyone serves Me, he must follow Me; and where I am, there My servant will be also; if anyone serves Me, the Father will honor him." At any rate, it is Christ who will send the Holy Spirit into the one soul trusting in Him that makes the born-again experience.

Second, Born Again is Not Reformation

I asked a Muslim woman why she wore a hijab, unlike before. She replied, "I am born again, to borrow your Christian teaching." The common understanding about the second birth is reformation. If you were a drunkard, for example, but changed your ways after realizing its dangers, your church would say you have had a born-again experience. This understanding is far from biblical. The second birth is a transformation or a divine intervention in your soul, a spiritual birth! It is not a U-turn to God's ways by man's superb morality or perfect righteousness.

Reformation's concept is comparable to remolding a pot using the same cart of mud. Your church can sculpt you to behave like a child of God, like a drunk guy pretending a decent poise. But if born again is a package, for example, reformation is not a part of that package. Wrote Paul that before your rebirth or regeneration, "you were dead in your trespasses and sins, in which you formerly walked according to the course of this world, according to the prince of the power of the air, of the spirit that is now working in the sons of disobedience." We "formerly lived in the lusts of our flesh, indulging the desires of the flesh and of the mind, and were by nature children of wrath." (Eph. 2:2-3) A tumbled stone is just a cleaned piece of banded amethyst or agate, and not a precious gem like a blue sapphire or diamond. It is how reformation works. It is a new life with no spiritual force as the rebirth required by Christ. Reformed we may be, but still unforgiven and dead in our sins. We need the second birth, not reformation!

One pastor left the Christian faith, for example, and shared in his blog how an old church member hugged him after delivering his sermon about the good God allowing intense suffering among the people. This preacher got a Ph.D. in Christian education and yet he was complaining he couldn't understand a good God bringing miseries to multitudes. This is one model of a Christian minister who is not born of God. For you don't even need a college education to see how good God was during the Exodus, and how blatantly unbelieving the Israelites were because of sin despite the tons of divine miracles.

The reformed heart is not the new heart and spirit that is saved from demonic darkness and deception. The Holy Spirit will teach us all things unless we don't have a born-again experience. Our God is not the Author of confusion as what the pastor we mentioned above had obviously suffered from. He left the faith because he had no scriptural faith, to begin with.

Paul tells us in Ephesians 2 that "God, being rich in mercy, because of His great love with which He loved us, even when we were dead in our transgressions, made us alive together with Christ (by grace you have been saved), and raised us up with Him, and seated us with Him in the heavenly places in Christ Jesus, so that in the ages to come He might show the surpassing riches of His grace in kindness toward us in Christ Jesus." (Eph. 2:4-7) We learned from this Scripture that it was God who made us alive together with Christ after Paul's declaration that we were dead in our trespasses and sins. It was God Himself who transformed us in Christ, not just reformed us as what most people assumed to be the meaning of the second birth.

Third, Born Again is Not Baptism or Church Membership

Baptism and church membership follow the born-again experience. But they don't produce rebirth in us by doing them.

A Catholic who's meeting Christ's Spirit by faith will leave Catholicism for "THEY SHALL ALL BE TAUGHT OF GOD" that idolatry is sin. (John 6:45) The baptized Catholic, always a Catholic punch line, makes little sense. Those church members from any Christian denomination who are not born of God are pseudo-Christians, and they devour gladly every false teaching fed to them.

We've discussed somewhere that born again is just synonymous with the biblical doctrine about our soul's salvation. It is the key to our entrance into God's kingdom, said our Lord. But it is not about baptism or church membership.

How is Born Again Related to Baptism?

Wrote the apostle Paul that "Christ did not send me to baptize, but to preach the gospel." (1 Cor. 1:17) The Gospel saves if we accept and believe it, but not baptism. (Rom. 1:16) That is why Christ sent Paul to preach, not to baptize.

Baptism represents the Gospel that Christ died and rose from the grave according to the Scriptures. (See 1 Cor. 15:1-4) If you believe in Christ, you won't hesitate to proclaim your faith in the Gospel through your baptism, which is a depiction, as mentioned above, of Christ's death, burial, and resurrection. (See Rom. 6:3-4)

I heard a man who wanted baptized to wash away his sins. A colossal blunder because water (gather all from the ocean!) can never save a soul. No forgiveness takes place for bathing. It is Christ's blood that saves. (1 John 1:7)

One pastor said in a debate that baptism saves a soul. "Is the candidate for baptism saved?" His opponent asked him. "No," he replied. Then came a follow-up question: "Is he saved after baptism?" "Yes," he answered. This guy's doctrine is that water saves. But we cannot find that from the Scriptures.

The defenders of the baptism-saves heresy use Mark 16:16 to prove their belief. Christ said: "He who has believed and has been baptized shall be saved; but he who has disbelieved shall be condemned." We find this Scripture only in Mark, but Jamieson-Fausset-Brown Bible Commentary[16] compares this verse with Romans 10:10-11.

It says: "Baptism is here put for the external signature of the inner faith of the heart, just as 'confessing with the mouth' is in Ro 10:10; and there also as here this outward manifestation, once mentioned as the proper fruit of faith, is not repeated in what follows (Ro 10:11)." The point is that baptism follows as the "external signature of the inner faith of the heart," but it is faith that saves since Christ said, "he who has disbelieved shall be condemned." The second part of the verse does not mention the lack of baptism, as baptism only follows faith. There is no hint that the unbaptized thief on the cross failed to enter Paradise!

For the faith that saves, Barnes holds that when a man understands he is a sinner and God's judgment awaits him after this life, he "would act on the belief of this truth and

---

[16] Jamieson-Fausset-Brown Bible Commentary. Mark 16:16. https://biblehub.com/commentaries/mark/16-16.htm (accessed November 10, 2020)

repent."

Barnes explained further the act of faith in this way: "The Lord Jesus died to save man. To have faith in Christ is to believe that this is true, and to act accordingly; that is, to trust him, to rely on him, to love him, to feel that we have no merit, and to cast our all upon him." (See Barnes Notes on the Holy Bible on Mark 16:16)

Those who believed that salvation requires water baptism also believed that baptism is a part of the Gospel. Christ said, "Go therefore and make disciples of all the nations, baptizing them." (Matt. 28:19a) We can divide the Great Commission into three subpoints, which are (1) going; (2) making disciples; and (3) baptizing those already discipled. In this instruction, the soul's salvation happens in subpoint two, which is disciple-making. Then follows baptism after conversion. From here, baptism is not a part of salvation but a symbol of faith in the Gospel. Wrote Barnes "No man can be saved without that regenerated and purified heart of which baptism is the appropriate symbol."

We also find the order of salvation and baptism in Acts 16. "Sirs, what must I do to be saved?" asked the Philippian jailer. "Believe in the Lord Jesus," Paul and Silas answered, "and you will be saved." Did Paul include baptism to get salvation? No. What did the Bible say in verse 32? "And they spoke the word of the Lord to him together with all who were in his house. And he took them that very hour of the night and washed their wounds, and immediately he was baptized, he and all his household." (Acts 16:30-32) Baptism follows salvation as a badge of faith in the Gospel that Christ died, entombed, and resurrected, thus confirming all His claims.

Baptismal regeneration is the phrase used for the teaching that baptism is a part of salvation. Since the Bible is the inspired Word of God, any perceived contradiction from its teachings requires a conclusive examination. It is an established theological precept that salvation is God's gift to man, and the latter is not a part of it except to accept and believe the gift. "For God so loved the world, that He gave His only begotten Son [Jesus], that whoever believes in Him shall not perish, but have eternal life. For by grace you have been saved through faith; and that not of yourselves, it is the gift of God; not as a result of works, so that no one may boast." (John 3:16; Eph. 2:8-9) Salvation is a gift of God and not a result of self-righteousness or good deeds.

We should resolve any Scripture contradicting the doctrine of salvation by grace through faith alone since our God does not contradict Himself. We consider First Peter 3:21 as a verse needing clarification. "Corresponding to that," Peter said, "baptism now saves you—not the removal of dirt from the flesh, but an appeal to God for a good conscience—through the resurrection of Jesus Christ."

Here is how gotquestions.org explains 1 Peter 3:21: "Baptism is not necessary for salvation. Baptism does not save from sin but from a bad conscience. In 1 Peter 3:21, Peter clearly taught that baptism was not a ceremonial act of physical purification, but the pledge of a good conscience toward God. Baptism is the symbol of what has already occurred in the heart and life of one who has trusted Christ as Savior (Romans 6:3-5; Galatians 3:27; Colossians 2:12). Baptism is an important step of obedience that every Christian should take. Baptism cannot be a requirement for salvation. To make it such is an attack on the sufficiency of the death and resurrection of Jesus Christ."[17]

---

[17] "Is baptism necessary for salvation? Gotquestions.org. "https://www.gotquestions.org/baptism-salvation.html (accessed December 5, 2020).

"Those who believe that baptism is required for salvation are quick to use 1 Peter 3:21 as a 'proof text,' because it states 'baptism now saves you.' Was Peter really saying that the act of being baptized is what saves us? If he were, he would be contradicting many other passages of Scripture that clearly show people being saved (as evidenced by their receiving the Holy Spirit) prior to being baptized or without being baptized at all. A good example of someone who was saved before being baptized is Cornelius and his household in Acts 10. We know that they were saved before being baptized because they had received the Holy Spirit, which is the evidence of salvation (Romans 8:9; Ephesians 1:13; 1 John 3:24). The evidence of their salvation was the reason Peter allowed them to be baptized. Countless passages of Scripture clearly teach that salvation comes when one believes in the gospel, at which time he or she is sealed 'in Christ with the Holy Spirit of promise' (Ephesians 1:13)."[18]

Now, how is born again related to baptism? Well, all born-again Christians submitted to water baptism as a part of our Christian duties, and we are not ashamed to proclaim our love for Jesus and the Gospel story depicted in baptism, which is Christ's burial and resurrection. (See Mark 8:38; Rom. 6:3-4)

How is Born Again Related to Church Membership?

Church membership, according to the Bible, follows salvation or the born-again experience. Luke wrote. "And the Lord was adding to their number day by day those who were being saved." (Acts 2:47) Christ added those saved to the membership of the church. He didn't add those who are not

---

[18] "Does 1 Peter 3:21 teach that baptism is necessary for salvation?" gotquestions.org.
https://www.gotquestions.org/baptism-1Peter-3-21.html (accessed December 5, 2020).

born again. The fake Christians are members of the physical organization of the local church (like a membership with a homeowners' association), but not a part of the body of Christ, the saved and Spirit-indwelt members of the Lord's Church.

Let's retrace: Church membership does not save a soul from God's wrath in hell. The false Christian leaders connect church membership to one's salvation. But the Bible does not teach it. The Catholic Church's control over the soul is baseless. Christ did not establish the church to save a soul, because He is the only Savior of man. The pope's claim as "Vicar of Christ" is blasphemous, since "vicar" means "to stand in place of Christ," but our Lord sent to us His Spirit to teach us all things. He does not need the pope to act as His replacement. Confession of sins to the sinful priest, therefore, is simply wrong. The church and her ministers cannot save a soul from hell, as they cannot forgive sins the way Christ did by shedding His own blood.

Judas' entrance in Christ's first crowd of disciples typifies the membership of the unsaved and false Christians in the churches today. The prophets saw Judas and prophesied about him. (See Ps. 109:8; Zech. 11:12-13) The Body of Christ, His Church, however, does not include those who are not born again. They are tares sowed by God's enemy among the wheat. (Matt. 13:25)

Most cults get their followings from the lure named church membership. To exteriorize the ploy to attract more members, cults' con artists would put more fixations on the church building's engaging architecture and uniformity.

We have seen most cults' church buildings under similar designs, giving the group a brand of sorts. This drive for identity and organization is part of the works of the flesh written in Galatians 5:20, which includes faction, division, or grouping.

True, the Evangelicals have also the drive for establishing organizations and groupings, but not for effecting the born-again requirement of Christ to enter God's kingdom. Church membership cannot save. The born-Catholic-die-Catholic trademark does not have a Bible connection.

How is born again related to church membership? Well, the assembly of born-again Christians glorifies our God. In the Scriptures, church, from the Greek word ecclesia, means many things. It can be a mob, the children of Israel, the body of Christ, etc. In this discussion, we want to focus on the assembly of the Christians in the local setting (1 Cor. 1:2; 2 Cor. 1:1; Gal. 1:1-2.) and the body of individual living believers (1 Cor. 15:9; Gal. 1:13)

I read somewhere about a genuine Christian who lived far away from the nearest Church. What he did was put a bench under a tree facing a river and a thick forest. Before returning home in the evening as a farmer, he would sit on his wooden bench to read his Bible, pray, and sing hymns to the Lord. He worshipped Jesus alone!

A born-again Christian is a churchgoer, but the four corners of his church cannot limit his worship of Christ.

What is the church's significance for the born-again believer of our Lord? Well, God adheres to the principles of growth. He needs 100 days to harvest corn or 30 years to mature a Ginkgo Biloba tree. The born-again Christian must undergo a process of growth, and the church helps him grow in the grace and knowledge of our Lord and Savior Jesus Christ. (2 Pet. 3:18) Without involvement with a church, we would not know how to encourage and build one another in the Lord.

The common problem with some church scenarios for the genuine believer is too much scholarship and pop-culture addiction by the preacher and his associates. Modernism buries the old-time religion. Instead of the singing of traditional hymns during worship in a genuine Baptist setting, for example, the ministers of the present-day culture introduce songs and the praise and worship deviation to imitate somehow the Charismatics' love for what is worldly entertainment. Instead of pursuing what is decent, holy, and biblical worship to our Father God, most junior ministers prefer to imitate what is trending on YouTube. Second, Christ's exaltation shrinks in the sermons of the modern pulpiteers, because of the Liberal's unscriptural inputs we find sinking the Internet. The Internet- and PowerPoint-dependent preachers are the most tiresome to listen to during a worship service. Third, the genuine born-again Christians always find objectionable the preacher's attempt to convert the church into a seminary classroom where he could whip his members with his scholarly Greek and Hebrew translations of the Bible. Without complete dependence upon God's Spirit, too much scholarship in the pulpit only starves the born-again Christians.

When the Holy Spirit stands over the church, the born-again believers would queue to hear the Sunday sermon. The Spirit's unction just doesn't happen these days as when Moody preached the Bible, so the born-again Christians must have a plan B to meet their spiritual needs.

I've been reading and writing about Spurgeon's teaching on secret devotion and implemented it together with my wife, and it worked for us for long years already. Wrote the apostle Paul in Galatians 1:13: "For you have heard of my former manner of life in Judaism, how I used to persecute the church of God beyond measure and tried to destroy it." Paul talked about the church of God without reference to a location as when he said, "To the church of God which is at Corinth." The word "ecclesia" was used in this instance as "the body of individual living believers." When Paul persecuted the church, he meant he persecuted every believer of Christ he knew of from different locations. That said, I am touching on God's action to strengthen us spiritually as born-again Christians by doing a secret devotion in the family setting. After waking up in the morning, my wife and I prayed together to our dear Lord and did it for over 30 years now. We based this devotion on the Bible's teaching from Matthew 18:19-20, where the church's total membership is reduced to two. Observe the word of our Lord:

> "Again I say to you, that if two of you agree on earth about anything that they may ask, it shall be done for them by My Father who is in heaven. For where two or three have gathered together in My name, I am there in their midst."

Fourth, Born Again is Not the Ability to Perform Miracles

Don't get me wrong. I believe in miracles and reject dispensationalism, which teaches that miracles do not belong to the church age. C.I. Scofield, its originator, erred somehow. I believe in miracles because Christianity is God's, and He works miracles! Observe Galatians 3:5: "I ask you again, does God give you the Holy Spirit and work miracles among you because you obey the law? Of course not! It is because you believe the message you heard about Christ." (NLT) The miracles of the Second Coming, the Virgin Birth, the Resurrection, among others, are the fundamentals of the Christian faith. Without faith in miracles, I don't have the binding authority to teach about the coming Rapture of the Saints.

Second, concerning wonders, God may do miracles at His pleasure; we just don't know. The preciseness of the laws of nature, for example, is mysterious, and God is maintaining the harmony of the physical world by His sheer omnipotence. Is it not a miracle that the distance of the earth away from the sun is simply perfect? Otherwise, had we been too far, we would have frozen up; or too close, burnt up!

Third, without faith in God's miracles in this dispensation, we cannot explain John 4:12, since Christ said: "Truly, truly, I say to you, he who believes in Me, the works that I do, he will do also; and greater works than these he will do; because I go to the Father."

What I Don't Believe in Today's Commercialized Miracles?

I don't believe, however, in commercialized miracles, like the miracles during a healing crusade with the clicking noises of the cameras that are processing videos for an HD YouTube upload.

I am writing this book during this Wuhan virus lockdown, but haven't heard of the popular miracle-working mega-church pastors driving out the pandemic from the hospitals and the marketplace. They are silent, like hiding away from the obvious evidence of their cover-ups.

Christ did not teach Nicodemus to perform a miracle to experience a rebirth. For those prophesying and doing miracles, our Lord said, "I never knew you." We find this teaching in Matthew 7 and verse 21, where Christ talked about the way to "enter the kingdom of heaven." It was the same topic Christ shared with Nicodemus in John 3 and verse 3. To enter God's kingdom, you need a second birth. Your skill in tongue-speaking, healing, and the casting out of demons won't impress God at all. By faith, Christ will fill you with the Holy Spirit, even without subscribing to the suspicious and pentecostalized signs and wonders. The born-again experience is a sign of salvation and forgiveness. We need not roll and crawl on the church floor to live in heaven forever.

Matthew chapter seven taught us that all forms of a miracle performed by the miracle workers don't guarantee salvation and eternal life.

One can be born again without the ability to do signs and wonders like speaking in tongues and other popular doctrines of the charismatized Christianity.

Fifth, Born Again is Not Unbelief

The fake Christians are unsaved members of the local church. They are the avowed doubters and atheists pretending Christianity. They sneaked into the church by baptism.

I am a student of unbelief if it is proper to call it that way since I love to know more about the attributes of the pseudo-Christians. Aside from their silent rejection of Christ and lack of hope for immortality, I learned also of their prayerlessness and lack of victory in life. All these dangerous symptoms of the Christian counterfeits and pretenders would reveal themselves during a severe trial. An old woman, for example, invited her pastor to pray over her sick daughter. After the prayer, the fever did not leave the young child contrary to the "miracle" expected by her mother. The pastor then left her house. But worried about her daughter, the old woman went to her idols, which she hid away after her baptism. It is the character of unbelief. The fake Christians don't trust in Jesus sincerely. Christ is not their Lord!

We have settled somewhere in this paper the truth that Christ made plain in John 3:16 His instruction to Nicodemus in John 3:3. After our Lord reasoned about the need for a rebirth to enter heaven, He taught that God "gave His only begotten Son [Jesus], that whoever believes in Him shall not perish, but have eternal life." To be born again, therefore, is to trust and rely upon the Son of God. Born again is acceptance, not a rejection of Christ.

In the Christian realm, unbelief hides in diverse ways. When a Christian supports Darwinism, for example, he is rejecting the truth that God created all things. He is embracing the theory of evolution, which is not biblical. He is an unbeliever. Paul said, "For by Him [Jesus] all things were created, both in the heavens and on earth, visible and invisible, whether thrones or dominions or rulers or authorities—all things have been created through Him and for Him." (Col. 1:16) A born-again Christian cannot be a Darwinist at the same time.

Some so-called Christians are teaching things strange as "dancing with the Spirit" because of unbelief. The other cause is the belief in the wrong Jesus. Observe this prayer posted on Facebook: "Lord, I Release Blessing from heaven. I Release Healing from Heaven. I Release Anointing from Heaven. I bring heaven to earth." It is God who will release everything through Christ from heaven—not your pastor! But those not born of God got thrilled with all things unscriptural.

Observe Acts 9:17:

"Brother Saul, the Lord Jesus, who appeared to you on the road by which you were coming, has sent me so that you may regain your sight and be filled with the Holy Spirit."

Christ used Ananias that Paul may regain his sight and that he may be filled with the Holy Spirit. It is not a sound teaching to say, "I released Anointing from Heaven" as if the pastor is playing God or taking the role of Jesus since he is more gifted or prayerful, or holier than the other members of the congregation.

Such power to "bring heaven to earth" is just a close cousin to the common "Christ spoke to me in my hotel!" doctrinal big talk.

If you are filled with the Holy Spirit for service (for example, teaching or preaching), you will radiate the power of God the Spirit for the salvation of souls. It happened as with D. L. Moody, Spurgeon, Wesley, Charles Finney, or George Whitefield in their work to win souls for Jesus. But no one among these famous preachers has claimed he had released to the congregants everything belonging to God alone.

"The sermons were not different," said D. L. Moody after experiencing the anointing of the Holy Spirit, "I did not present any new truths, and yet hundreds were converted."

The Holy Spirit will flow out of your body like "rivers of living water" through Christ and by Him alone since the anointing of the Spirit is possible only with Christ's exaltation and authority. Said Christ in Luke 24:49: "And behold, I am sending forth the promise of My Father upon you; but you are to stay in the city until you are clothed with power from on high." Christ Himself will give you the fullness of the Holy Spirit for service—and not for ecstatic "dancing or laughing with the Holy Spirit!" If the preacher would "Release Anointing from heaven," it would redound to his glorification, not Christ's. Our jealous God won't allow it.

Observe John 7:37-39:

"Now on the last day, the great day of the feast, Jesus stood and cried out, saying, 'If anyone is thirsty, let him come to Me and drink. He who believes in Me, as the Scripture said, "From his innermost being will flow rivers of living water."' But this He spoke of the Spirit, whom those who believed in Him were to receive; for the Spirit was not yet given, because Jesus was not yet glorified."

Let's reiterate. The fullness or anointing of the Holy Spirit happens only after Christ's exaltation. The Jesus of this world (the other Jesus, and not the biblical Jesus) gives signs and wonders through his workers as what's happening in weird church's services posted on Facebook. For "false Christs and false prophets will arise, and will show signs and wonders, in order to lead astray, if possible, the elect." (Mark 13:22)

Christ gives us the indwelling and infilling of the Holy Spirit (not your miracle-performing pastor or deacon). The Bible does not mention the pastor or elder as the giver of God's Spirit. He cannot release Spirit's anointing from heaven!

Wrote Paul, "In Him [Jesus] you also, after listening to the message of truth, the gospel of your salvation—having also believed, you were sealed in Him with the Holy Spirit of promise, who is given as a pledge of our inheritance." (Eph. 1:13) The moment of your genuine conversion is the minute of the Holy Spirit's indwelling in your soul. Your faith causes Jesus to seal you with His Spirit. (Rom. 8:9)

But if your pastor or elder would say, "I release to you the Holy Spirit," we don't know from what divine source is he basing such an authority. He may be referring to the Holy Spirit's infilling, but the Spirit's fullness is given only by Christ for service and the salvation of the soul.

We see sad realities happening in the Churches today. For when the Christian doubts the Bible as the inspired Word of God, he would not doubt when fed with unscriptural teachings like the obsession for prosperity and signs and wonders. From there, the apostle John commanded us "not believe every spirit, but test the spirits to see whether they are from God, because many false prophets have gone out into the world." (1 John 4:1)

The born-again Christian is careful with his doctrines because the Holy Spirit will teach him all things. "These things I have written to you," said John, "concerning those who are trying to deceive you. As for you, the anointing which you received from Him abides in you, and you have no need for anyone to teach you; but as His anointing teaches you about all things." (1 John 2:26-27)

Sixth, Born Again is Not Prayerlessness

Another trait of a nominal Christian is the lack of a prayer life. When God required us to "pray without ceasing," He didn't mean a long-hour praying. Said C. H. Spurgeon: "While your hands are busy with the world, let your hearts still talk with God; not in twenty sentences at a time, for such an interval might be inconsistent with your calling, but in broken sentences and interjections. It is always wrong . . . running away to pray at all hours; but we may, without this, let short sentences go up to heaven."[19]

But the false Christian cannot see the value of prayer to the Christ of the Scriptures, be it a long or short prayer! One reason is that Jesus is not his Savior and Lord. He is not born again.

I never cease to pray after meeting Jesus in my heart in 1984, over 36 years ago. I experienced a connection with God—I prayed in the back of my mind wherever I go, aside from my morning devotion together with my wife. The tip of my tongue and the lips of my heart talked to Jesus and praise His name countless times a day. Jesus is my Everything. He is my Sustainer, Provider, my Health, and my Life—He's All for me! I would feel uneasy about driving a car without saying my prayers first. Prayer is just like food for the soul of the genuine born-again Christian. The fake ones don't have such a praying passion and spontaneity. Christ is not their Lord and God!

During Christ's incarnation (when He was human like us),

---

[19] Blue Letter Bible. "C. H. Spurgeon: 'Pray Without Ceasing'". blueletterbible.org.
https://www.blueletterbible.org/Comm/spurgeon_charles/sermons/103 9.cfm (accessed November 15, 2020).

"He went off to the mountain to pray, and He spent the whole night in prayer to God." (Luke 6:12) "In the days of His flesh," states Hebrews 5:7, "He offered up both prayers and supplications with loud crying and tears." Praying to the Father in Heaven through Christ is just how the genuine Christian ought to live because the prayer of the upright is God's delight. (Prov. 15:8b)

When you are prayerless, therefore, you are a Christian without experiencing a rebirth. But don't worry. You still have time to repent of your unbelief and trust Jesus.

I had a relative-in-law who asked me why God gave her kidney disease. As she breathed the labored or agonal breathing before her death, I shared with her Jesus and the eternal life He promised. She kept on praying and murmuring the word "JESUS" before her death. Later, I discovered a smile painted on her lips. What happened? She saw Jesus while her soul left her? Maybe. Because prayer works.

Seventh, Born Again is Not Rejection of the Bible

It is easy to spot the fake believers during a Bible study session, for example. For they don't take the Word of God seriously. When the angels ordered Lot and his family not to turn to look back, Lot's wife looked back, ignoring the angels' instruction—rejecting the Word of God! I met people in a Bible class interested in the time and format of the study instead of dissecting God's word verse by verse like anatomizing a frog bone by bone. In my heart, I want to "eat" the word of God—I desire Christ to speak to me through His Word.

Technology is now aiding Christians with the audio Bible. I always listen to God talking to me as I do my exercises in the morning with my smartphone's audio Bible nearby. "You foolish Galatians, who has bewitched you (Cf. Gal. 3:1)," I can feel the heartbeat of God. "Woe, woe, woe to those who dwell on the earth (See Rev. 8:13, NASB) I can see His righteous wrath. "O generation of vipers, how can ye, being evil, speak good things?" (Matt. 12:34) I can feel the heart of Jesus against those leaders of unbelief. But the fake Christians don't have this deep affection for the blessed Word of God. Their repudiation of the authority and sacredness of the Holy Scriptures reveal their silent rejection of Jesus Christ.

From my book, "Christian Teachings Revisited," I wrote the following under the heading, TRUTH IS ABSOLUTE:

> I became a Christian by the grace of God. The first thing I thought was a great improvement to my character and being was my new attitude of giving God the glory in all my life's routine. God-centeredness (rather than self-centeredness) got its curve in me. The emptiness that lived like a resident in my heart vanished away as soon as I embraced my Christian faith. I was born again—Christ changed me. I found life's meaning—which I searched out for so long—at last. And it happened right after having met by faith the God of the Holy Bible, the God of truth, Christ our Lord. (John 14:6; 1:1; 14; Tit. 2:13)

> How did it happen? Why the miraculous change inside my soul? My answer is that when I learned about the Gospel, I believed it was the whole absolute truth; that Christ died for me and rose again to affirm my eternal life by His promises. Our Lord said, ". . . because I live, you will live also" (John 14:19b), and I believed it as the great, guaranteeing, and absolute truth for my soul. I believed in God's Word as the absolute truth and believed and obeyed what it told me, and the perturbation and emptiness inside me disappeared as the peace of Christ populated my soul. (Cf. John 14:27)

The Bible haters tried to sell their godless teachings to as many readers as they can reach through the Internet. All enemies of Christ must have been happy with their efforts to dethrone the God of the Scriptures. One anti-Bible blogger, for example, wrote that "the Bible would not be a guidebook for attaining human happiness and well-being. It would instead perpetuate the ideas of an ignorant and superstitious past—and prevent humanity from rising to a higher level." These atheists hate the Bible when it talks against sin and homosexuality, but want to use it at the same time to support their "brotherly love" teaching. Reason and secular thinking serve as their ultimate authority instead of the Holy Scriptures. Christ endorsed the Scriptures, but the Humanists and Liberal Theologians have more confidence in their belief system incompatible with the Word of God. They are not afraid to offend God since they don't believe He exists.

But here is the position of the born-again Christian concerning the Holy Bible as penned by J. C. Ryle:

"Here is a book written by a succession of Jews, in a little corner of the world, which positively stands alone. Not only where its writers isolated and cut off in a peculiar manner from other nations, but they belonged to a people who have never produced any other book of note except the Bible! There is not the slightest proof that, unassisted and left to themselves, they were capable of writing anything remarkable, like the Greeks and the Romans. Yet these men have given the world a volume which for depth, unity, sublimity, accuracy, suitableness to the wants of man, and power of influencing its readers, is perfectly unrivalled. How can this be explained? How can it be accounted for? To my mind there is only one answer. The writers of the Bible were divinely helped and qualified for the work which they did. The book which they have given to us was written by inspiration of God."[20]

Eighth, Born Again is Not Hopelessness

I have seen more hopeless people, from the greatest to the smallest of them, in many unfamiliar places in the world through social media, documentaries, and a few visits to unique cities abroad. But what is hope all about? Well, it is the confidence of a future good for the spiritual side of life. And when you don't have it, your soul will hunger for it. The subconscious mind craves for heaven and life beyond. Fanaticism and superstition developed out of hopelessness concerning eternity. As the image of God (Cf. 1 Cor. 11:7), we have a God-shaped void in our hearts, forming our inner struggles and emptiness. Despair breeds suicidal tendencies in some godless people. The apostle Paul said that outside of Christ, people have "no hope and without God in the world." (Eph. 2:12) Those having no born-again experience carry a Christless soul and a Spirit-less life. And the pseudo-Christians are just like that: No Jesus inside them—no spiritual hope of immortality!

The story of discontent and desperation from the last words of Steve Jobs and other men of wealth and fame speaks volumes about the hopelessness of the unbelievers of Jesus Christ. False Christians are just like the atheists who don't know who to call and where to go in the hour of sickness and the ensuing death. The pandemic of the hopelessness of humanity percolates into all cultures and classes of people. Both the rich and the poor, the ignorant and the learned ones, have desired the same divine armor from the power of death. And then Jesus came and offered immortality to all who trust in Him. The apostles of Christ, who succumbed to death as

---

[20] John Charles Ryle, Old Paths (The Banner of Truth Trust, Edinburgh, U.K., First Published, 1878, Reprinted 2005), 15.

martyrs, believed and died fearlessly because of the hope of eternal life from the promise of Christ, their Lord and God. Sad that the pseudo-Christians don't expect to live forever in heaven as they don't have the Spirit of Truth; they don't encounter the mystery of the second birth. What they have is the church, but not the Lord.

Here is how the apostle Paul explained hope because of the residence of the Holy Spirit in the born-again person: "[A]nd hope does not disappoint, because the love of God has been poured out within our hearts through the Holy Spirit who was given to us." (Rom. 5:5)

Ninth, Born Again is Not Helplessness

The other distinctive of a bogus Christian is the lack of victory over life's trials. One church pastor, for example, left the ministry to become a schoolteacher, and then an insurance underwriter, and finally, a tricycle driver—a story of an endless demotion! The apostle Paul underwent the same lowering of social status from a powerful Pharisee to an impoverished disciple of Christ. But he was not lacking in victory. He said in 2 Corinthians 2:14: "But thanks be to God, who always leads us in triumph in Christ, and manifests through us the sweet aroma of the knowledge of Him in every place." In Paul's experience, he equates the knowledge of Christ's presence in his trials as "the sweet aroma of the knowledge of Him." The false Christians, however, don't have "the knowledge of Him." They face their adversities alone, just like the other unbelievers. They don't have a victory in Christ since they don't involve Jesus in their ordeals.

Tenth, Born Again is Not Being Nicer

You can be nicer to people, even if you don't have a religion. Most politicians, for example, master the art of hanging around with people, rubbing elbows with them. Most of our acquaintances are pleasers of people. But their friendliness cannot pass as proof for the second birth experience.

I had a casual friend who donated millions to charity but got annoyed when I brought up Jesus Christ into the discussion. Doing good deeds to your neighbor is just not the way to enter the kingdom of God.

The born again teaching of Christ, which He taught during Nicodemus' night visit, involves 21 verses of Scripture. Part of this Sacred Instruction to get into God's kingdom is the famous John 3:16. And our Lord mentioned nothing about being nicer to live in heaven forever.

What Christ taught Nicodemus is about conversion. "Born Again" means a new birth into the household of God. It means you are a genuine believer and follower of Jesus. For "whoever believes in Him shall not perish, but have eternal life."

Does it mean the born-again Christians are bad at teamwork, boring, or easily annoyed when mingling with those non-born-again people around them? No. Those born of God are the best people to be teachers or TV anchors or politicians because Christ is our "wisdom from God." (Cf. 1 Cor. 1:30) God's Spirit will teach us all truth. (Cf. John 14:26)

Paul, however, said, "there must be no filthiness and silly talk, or coarse jesting, which are not fitting, but rather giving of thanks." (Eph. 5:4) It is expected among believers to behave differently. The result is people's impression that Christians are not nicer to them, as if the true followers of Jesus are out of this world. It is how the darkness condemns the light. For this worldly disgust against the Christians, Christ said: "If you were of the world, the world would love its own; but because you are not of the world, but I chose you out of the world, because of this the world hates you." (John 15:19) There is always tension between the believers and the unbelievers.

Can you imagine your exposure to risk as a Christian in the community of unbelievers? What is your future then, as a born-again Christian in a Muslim or ISIS-controlled territory?

From Christ's lips, He taught that "they will deliver you to tribulation, and will kill you, and you will be hated by all nations because of My name." (Matt. 24:9).

In my lost state, a pastor approached and taught me salvation through faith in Jesus. It was the most admirable thing that one Christian guy had ever done for my soul. I can never forget it.

Is the born-again Christian nicer than others? Yes, if you will listen to him because you can get salvation through his guidance and testimonies. However, if you will behave wickedly, he will crush your pride with his Bible verses and Christian doctrines. Such an offensive could never make you feel that the born-again Christian is someone likable.

7. WHAT BORN AGAIN IS?

*"But even if we, or an angel from heaven, preach
any other gospel to you than what we have
preached to you, let him be accursed."*
— Galatians 1:8.

WHEN NICODEMUS TOLD Jesus, "we know You," our Lord responded something like, "it is not enough, Nico! You must be born again." (See John 3:2-3)

In short, your knowledge of Christ means nothing to God. If you are not born again, you will wake up in hell as a Bible scholar, or whatever rank you may have in religion. You may memorize the entire Bible, read all the commentaries from the Internet, even if you are not born of the Spirit. Judas, for example, knew everything known to Christ's first disciples, but he was not one of them!

So, what is being born again?

Born Again is a Fixed Rule

You can be a Christian with no born-again experience. Christ's teaching, however, to enter God's kingdom by the second birth, is a fixed rule. It is like living in God's city with a Spirit-renewed heart as the sole passport or qualification. A Christian who is not born of God's Spirit cannot go there.

Born again means salvation from hell because you cannot enter God's kingdom without it. Life after death, therefore, is true because Christ taught it, even prescribed the method to live forever.

The natural belief system since time began is that one's

service to God and his neighbors guarantees blissful immortality. You need to be generous and do righteous deeds to inherit eternal life. Christ, however, shatters this false belief by saying only the second birth assures anyone entrance to God's home.

As a man loves to reinvent things, he tries to sway Christ's fixed rule by believing his money given to the church (as in Catholicism) may earn him forgiveness and everlasting life. Money, however, doesn't have value in God's ecosystem. To understand better the divine scenario, think of gold, which is just used for paving the streets of God's downtown. (Rev. 21:21)

Christ's born-again rule is fixed and we only need to apply it, instead of changing the rule.

As I write this paragraph, I am thinking of one unbeliever excited to enter God's kingdom by using the wrong address. If you want to live in heaven, use Christ's method, which is the second birth experience. The devil has hundreds of routes he used to enter God's city like baptism, church membership, obedience to the Law, and deeds of righteousness, but they are all deceptions for you to land in hell instead.

The safest address to heaven is Christ's address, which is the born-again experience. His rule to live forever is for one to be reborn by the Spirit of God. And this rule is fixed!

Born Again as Described in Romans 8:9

Our key text is John 3:3 where Christ said, "[U]nless one is born again he cannot see the kingdom of God." The apostle Paul, however, threw light on Christ's teaching from the angle of the Spirit's indwelling in the soul and body of Christ's genuine believers. "You are not in the flesh," wrote Paul, "but in the Spirit, if indeed the Spirit of God dwells in you. But if anyone does not have the Spirit of Christ, he does not belong to Him." (Rom. 8:9) In this Scripture, we find the "Spirit" (or the Holy Spirit), the "Spirit of God," and the "Spirit of Christ" living inside the person who believed, trusted, and relied upon Jesus Christ, the Son of God. The Triune God (God the Father, God the Son, and God the Spirit) live in your soul, thus working up in you the phenomenon we call the born-again experience.

Before you invited Christ to lord over your life, you were the sovereign owner and ruler of your mind and heart. You didn't pray to the God of the Holy Bible; you didn't love Jesus before! Now, you are a new person. Why? Because the Triune God did not sit on the throne of your heart to do nothing, but to transform you, to enlighten your darkened heart; to change and convert you, and to implant in you the born-again experience.

Born Again as Experienced by Paul

Saul persecuted the Lord's church. Later, he became the apostle Paul—he was born again!

When Christ ordered Ananias to help Paul regain his temporary blindness, Ananias reacted and said: "Lord, I have heard from many about this man, how much harm he did to Your saints . . . to bind all who call on Your name." (Acts 9:13-14) Paul himself affirmed his violent fanaticism with the Galatians by saying: "[You] have heard of my former manner of life in Judaism, how I used to persecute the church of God beyond measure and tried to destroy it." (Gal. 1:13) Then, Paul experienced the second birth after meeting Christ at a Damascus road, around two years after His resurrection.

The biblical metaphor used about spiritual rebirth is one's transformation from the experience of darkness to light. And Paul experienced it. In Colossians 1:13, He said, "For He rescued us from the domain of darkness, and transferred us to the kingdom of His beloved Son."

Hence, we don't just understand the born again doctrine, but experience with the works of the Holy Spirit in transforming us after an encounter with Jesus by faith!

In writing about the depravity of human nature, Dale Carnegie wrote about Francis "Two Gun" Crowley in the following terseness: "Without saying a word, Crowley drew his gun and cut the policeman down with a shower of lead. As the dying officer fell, Crowley leaped out of the car, grabbed the officer's revolver, and fired another bullet into the prostrate body. And that was the killer who said: "Under this coat is a weary heart, but a kind one—one that would do nobody any harm." Carnegie theorized we naturally think we are good, and we're always defensive to protect our self-esteem. In the language of the Scriptures, we are dead in our sins. We don't acknowledge our depraved nature.

Paul said we live in the domain of darkness.

Wrote the Apostle in Romans 1:22-23: "Professing to be wise, they became fools, and exchanged the glory of the incorruptible God for an image in the form of corruptible man and of birds and four-footed animals and crawling creatures." I followed a brilliant Catholic educator on Facebook who was an idol-worshiper. I unfollowed her after a while!

Before our second birth experience, the lusts and desires of our flesh, which the Bible describes as a kind of spiritual death, enslave us.

Now comes our rebirth in God's Spirit! How the new person in us turns up? How are we made new inwardly in our soul and heart? Paul explained: "But God, being rich in mercy, because of His great love with which He loved us, even when we were dead in our transgressions, made us alive together with Christ (by grace you have been saved)." (Eph. 2:4-5)

By His grace, God makes us alive from our spiritual death because of sin. By faith in Christ, our Redeemer, God gives us forgiveness, salvation, and eternal life in heaven.

We don't have a better description of a genuine rebirth than that it is a born-again experience foreign to all unbelievers.

Born Again Versus Other Teachings

The phrase "born again" came from Jesus Christ. No author or someone famous inventing it. Christ coined it. Our life after death lies in these two words. Said our Lord, "Truly, truly, I say to you, unless one is born again he cannot see the kingdom of God." We don't have the liberty to misunderstand it since it is the key to live forever—and it came from the lips of the Son of God Himself!

I studied the salvation teachings of Buddhism, Islam, and Hinduism. All of them preach good deeds to earn happy immortality or a more elevated identity, as with the Buddhist Reincarnation Doctrine.

But Christianity is far different. Good works don't save a soul. Our righteous deeds are impure in God's eyes. Wrote the prophet Isaiah: "For all of us have become like one who is unclean, And all our righteous deeds are like a filthy garment." (Is. 64:6) God cannot see any deed of righteousness from all the carnal peoples of the world. We need forgiveness and a redeemer. God is holy; we are not! Without a savior of sin, God burned Sodom and Gomorrah and flooded the entire world during Noah's time. Without a savior, God required the Jews a blood offering to appease His anger against sin and disobedience.

Three things explain the implication of the blood-sacrifice system as required by God. One is that life is in the blood. (Lev. 17:11) Since the penalty of sin is death, the blood offering reminds the Israelites of the bloody consequence of sinning against our Creator.

Second, God commanded the Israelites to sprinkle blood on their doorposts to protect themselves from the plague, for the Almighty "will strike down all the firstborn in the land of Egypt, both man and beast." (Ex. 12:12) The blood offering reminds us of salvation.

Third, the blood sacrifice typifies Christ's own blood, which He shed at Calvary to redeem humanity from sin. Observe 1 Peter 1:18-19: "[Knowing] that you were not redeemed with perishable things like silver or gold from your futile way of life inherited from your forefathers, but with precious blood, as of a lamb unblemished and spotless, the blood of Christ."

The heavenly Father gave Jesus, as a sacrifice for sin to give us free salvation by faith in His Son. "For God so loved the world, that He gave His only begotten Son, that whoever believes in Him shall not perish, but have eternal life."

Our God gave us a plan to enter heaven and live there forever, and it was the plan to be born again by trusting in Christ and His promises.

Tons of teachings on how to get saved and enter God's kingdom grow fast like poison weeds to choke Christ's born-again doctrine. The Muslims tell the world to pray five times for purification, while the Buddhists and Hindus teach the cycle of reincarnation. Buddhism also banks on its enlightenment doctrine as to man's ultimate achievement by having the right view, intention, speech, action, livelihood, effort, mindfulness, and right concentration. The pseudo-Christians preach their good deeds, church membership, and baptism as essential to receiving salvation from God's wrath. In all these plans for immortality, no involvement or intervention from the Holy Spirit of God. It is the marked difference in Christ's second birth teaching to enter God's kingdom. The world's religions (which includes the cultic and fake Christian denominations) are just so obsessed about what man can do to secure his blissful life in the hereafter. This faith system is man-made and man-dependent, and not Christ- and Spirit-transformed.

Born Again is a Spiritual Transformation

Transformation is a metamorphosis like a caterpillar to the pupa and the adult butterfly. Spiritual transformation is just as conspicuous as a worthless father becoming a loving and responsible family man after conversion to born-again Christianity.

In 2nd Corinthians 5:17, the apostle Paul said, "Therefore if anyone is in Christ, he is a new creature; the old things passed away; behold, new things have come." The second birth is a distinct and real experience. Paul wrote about it from his radical persecute-the-Church crusade to his plant-Christian-churches campaigns throughout the known world. Such was a caterpillar to butterfly metamorphosis. No one can deny Paul's spiritual U-turn.

The great Apostle listed love, joy, patience, etc. as the fruit of the Spirit. Then in Galatians 5:24, he said: "Now those who belong to Christ Jesus have crucified the flesh with its passions and desires." Somewhere, Paul also said that our Lord will intervene to strengthen His followers and give them victory in this demon-dominated world.

God ensures the progress of our spiritual transformation since He said, "I will never desert you, nor will I ever forsake you." (Heb. 13:5)

Once a born-again Christian is always a born-again Christian. Otherwise, our God would become weak and unable to keep His children away from the strikes of the evil one. For the incorrigible backsliders, the Bible said they left us because they don't really belong to us. (Cf. 1 John 2:19) The Holy Spirit did not transform them.

Born Again Means Two Births and One Death

God saves us from His wrath and judgment if we have the second birth experience, for the Scripture teaches that "there is now no condemnation for those who are in Christ Jesus." (Rom. 8:1)

If we don't strive to have two births, which is equivalent to our salvation from hell, it could mean we are unconsciously trying to meet two deaths. One is death in the grave, and the second is death in hell.

A deathless life in hell is also called the second death. We find this in Revelation 20:14: "Then death and Hades were thrown into the lake of fire. This is the second death, the lake of fire."

If God would give me one hundred lives, I would spend all my waking hours figuring out how to continue living after the deadline. Death is not a part of our subconsciousness because God created Adam and Eve as immortal beings. We don't prepare to die, and neither do we prepare to meet God. We are not mindful of death, and dying twice never crosses our minds.

It is the greatest tragedy in life for one to never think about dying one day and facing God's judgment, given our sinfulness and imperfections.

The born-again phenomenon, therefore, is always worthy of our sincerest attention.

Born Again Thrives on the Bible's Inspiration

The true second birth experience can take place only after one realizes the authority of the Holy Scriptures. The Liberal Theology teaches that Christianity should not be based on "external authority," since it rejects the doctrine of the Bible's inerrancy and inspiration. No one can enter God's kingdom without faith in the Holy Scripture as the "divine revelation, the original autographs of which were verbally inspired by the Holy Spirit."

Why is it impossible for the doubters of the Bible to experience rebirth? The answer is that the salvation of our souls, which we also refer to as the born-again experience in this book, happens only after exercising faith in the Scripture as the Word of God. Wrote Paul: "For I am not ashamed of the gospel, for it is the power of God for salvation to everyone who believes." (Rom. 1:16) The Gospel saves, there is power in it to "everyone who believes." James also said, "in humility receive the word implanted, which is able to save your souls." (James 1:21b) The Holy Spirit won't work in the souls of those rejecting the Bible's authority.

It happened with the two Disciples of Christ who departed to a village named Emmaus because of unbelief. The risen Jesus then accompanied them (our Lord prevented them from recognizing Him) and explained to them as they walked the scripturalness of His death and resurrection. Wrote Luke: "Then beginning with Moses and with all the prophets, He explained to them the things concerning Himself in all the Scriptures." (Luke 24:27) After Jesus left them, "they said to one another, 'Were not our hearts burning within us while He was speaking to us on the road, while He was explaining the Scriptures to us?'" (v.32) We can gather important lessons from this biblical account. First, Christ honored the entire Scriptures (beginning with Moses and with all the prophets!). He discussed His death and resurrection based on solid biblical evidence. Second, the Holy Spirit touched the disciples' hearts as Christ preached to them the Scriptures. These doubters could not have decided to return to Jerusalem after their encounter with the risen Jesus, had they thought the Liberals' theology of the errancy and unreliability of the Bible. But, no! They returned to Jerusalem, to the group of John and Peter, fast as a rabbit since they believe in the Scriptures as the inspired or God-breathed Word of God.

I want to share a quote from my book, "Overcoming Adversities by the Power of God," concerning God's letter to man, which is the Holy Bible.

"The predominant Orthodox Christian Theology always defends the divine inspiration of the Holy Bible. True Christianity grows only by a right view of the Bible as God-breathed! Asserted the apostle Paul: "All Scripture is breathed out by God and profitable for teaching, for reproof, for correction, and for training in righteousness" (2 Tim. 3:16, ESV).

"No single book on Earth (aside from the Bible) tells God's words in the first person like 'I am the God of Abraham,' etc. The divine authority of the Scriptures is seen quickly as when Genesis 1:1 states: 'In the beginning God created the heavens and the earth.' The Holy Spirit who inspired and guided the writing of the Scriptures assumed that all people would believe in God instinctively since they knew God (Cf. Rom. 1:19-21); they were created in His image (Gen. 1:27). The Scriptures prove that unbelief in the Bible, in the context of liberalism, is a false Christianity (Read: John 5:39-40).

"Have you noticed any introduction in the first sentence when our Creator first entered the threshold of the written word? Did not God instead say in Genesis 1:1: 'In the beginning, before the world began, there was a supreme being who was omnipotent, omniscient, and omnipresent, who was called God. He was uncreated, and no power or being was greater than Him, and there was not a single mighty being before

Him'? God did not give His 'ID,' so to speak, or sort of 'About Page.' He simply said: 'In the beginning God created the heavens and the earth.' Observe the statement 'Thus saith the Lord,' on the pages of the King James Version of the Bible. (See Is. 45:1, etc.) All these verify just one awesome truth—the inspiration of the Holy Scriptures.

"Wrote J. C. Ryle: 'Begin to read it [the Scriptures] this very day. What greater insult to God can a man be guilty of than to refuse to read the letter God sends him from heaven? Oh, be sure, if you will not read your Bible, you are in fearful danger of losing your soul . . .. Let us hear the conclusion of the whole matter. God has given us the Bible to be a light to guide us to everlasting life. Let us not neglect this precious gift. Let us read it diligently, walk in its light, and we shall be saved.'"[21]

As the infant relies on the mother's milk, so the born-again person relies on the Bible's authority. The Liberals reject the Bible's inspiration, and no one can save them since even Christ Himself used the Scriptures to validate His claims. The false Christian rejects the Bible's whip hand. He is following Jesus, but from the wrong direction, since he does not have the light, which is the Word of God. As such, he is blinded by the devil, a Christian who is unsaved and hell-bound.

But God is love. He always gives chance to the Bible mockers until His patience wears out as with those laughing at Noah. "For as in those days before the flood," said Christ, "they were eating and drinking, marrying and giving in marriage, until the day that Noah entered the ark, and they did not understand until the flood came and took them all away." (Matt. 24:38-39b)

---

21 John Charles Ryle, Old Paths (The Banner of Truth Trust, Edinburgh, U.K., First Published, 1878, Reprinted 2005), 31;35.

Born Again Means Salvation

Our soul's salvation from hell is Christ's central message. He desires our safety after death since our unsaved soul will face judgment and the wrath of God if we don't have a born-again experience. We are valuable, according to our Lord—even more valuable than the entire world. Christ said, "For what will it profit a man if he gains the whole world and forfeits his soul? Or what will a man give in exchange for his soul?" (Matt. 16:26) In this verse, our Lord just talked about one man versus the value of the world, and not the 7.5 billion global population as a flock. Can we imagine the wealth of the U.S., Canada, and other countries? But God treasured our souls more because this world is passing away, while we will live eternally either for bliss or woe. Spurgeon said both God and the devil are interested of our soul. That's how important our soul is!

Our souls' salvation is the one thing we don't know of and don't care about. We want the material, and not the spiritual, side of things. I knew of someone whose confidence in his tough health at age 60 radiates in his words, even while undergoing a serious medical checkup. But, when he learned from his doctor, he had only two months to live, his proud I-am-healthy mindset melted away like salt in water. He knew he would soon die. His remaining 60 days are crucial for survival. He needed what we call "salvation."

The natural man cannot see the life after death promised by Christ. His option is to reject the Scriptures until someone preached to him the Gospel. Taught the apostle Paul: "How then will they call on Him in whom they have not believed? How will they believe in Him whom they have not heard? And how will they hear without a preacher?" (Rom. 10:14)

Your salvation from hell happens under two conditions: First, is faith in Christ, and second, faith in the Bible as the

Word of God. But you cannot believe without the help of a preacher or someone sent by God. Wrote the apostle Paul: "How will they preach unless they are sent?" (Rom. 10:15)

One devout Muslim teacher discovered she had a rare disease, which baffled all her physicians. Desperate, she went to her Christian friend, her fellow teacher, for a prayer. Long story short, she got healed and became a Christian. It is an instance of a born-again teacher sharing the Gospel and God honored what she did. She was a teacher, not a preacher, but it does not matter because preaching is explaining or proclaiming. Some Bible translations even use the word "telling" instead of preaching.

Some said you cannot preach with authority if you are not sent by a church. The Scripture used to support this claim is Romans 10:15. "How will they preach unless they are sent?"

This claim is false because Christ commissions all born-again Christians to preach by His authority. Observe Matthew 28:18-19: And Jesus came up and spoke to them, saying, "All authority has been given to Me in heaven and on earth. Go therefore and make disciples of all the nations, baptizing them in the name of the Father and the Son and the Holy Spirit, teaching them to observe all that I commanded you; and lo, I am with you always, even to the end of the age." Yes, disciple-making is not just the work of the pastor if we equate the word preacher to pastor exclusively.

Here is how Paul explains Romans 10:15 in First Corinthians if we trust that the best commentary of the Scripture is the Scripture itself:

"Now we ["we" means brethren or all born-again Christians, not just the pastors!] have received, not the spirit of the world, but the Spirit who is from God, so that we may know the things freely given to us by God, which things we also speak, not in words taught by human wisdom, but in those taught by the Spirit, combining spiritual thoughts with spiritual words." (1 Cor. 2:12-13) In short, we preach, proclaim, or share to the unbelievers "the things freely given to us by God . . . the things we also speak."

When Paul said you cannot preach unless you are sent, it means, unless the Spirit of God sent you. A person sharing the Good News without God's anointing is just lecturing and giving stories that don't touch the soul.

Faith in Christ and the Holy Scriptures require both the Holy Spirit and the Spirit-filled gospeller.

As a young preacher 30 years ago, I found Proverbs 14:12 as my easy pick for a text when called upon to preach unprepared. It says in King James Version: "There is a way which seemeth right unto a man, but the end thereof are the ways of death." I love this Scripture, for I want my audience to see that without Christ's Spirit in our soul—without the born-again experience—all our ways would only lead us to the cemetery and then to hell. All our efforts; all our miseries or celebrations would only come together into that lake of fire, which is the second death. "The grave attracts our feet, and we are moving to that direction and getting there soon, like it or not," runs my invented wisdom tip. I need to open the hearts of my listeners by the power of the Holy Spirit's intervention to understand their need for salvation.

Someone said that the first solution to a problem is the acceptance that the problem exists. Only when a man perceives his lost condition and his impending plunge into hell, should he die unsaved and unforgiven can he crave for his salvation and forgiveness. Until they see their need for salvation from the wrath of God because of sin, people don't cling to Christ for help. Sin makes us lost sinners in this world. We need to acknowledge it and then fix it!

One person rejected the Gospel presented by his Christian

friend for two years, but then the former got converted elsewhere and became a serious Bible student. One day he met his Christian friend again, and he sounded chiding with the question: "Why didn't you give me a rough shake in my head when I first rejected Jesus? What do you think would have had happened had I died unsaved?"

Salvation is urgent since death is unpredictable. Some died very old age, but others don't have the same opportunity. Mozart, for example, died at 35. A short or long life does not matter with God, however, for as long as you are already at the age of accountability. At that age, you need to get salvation! John MacArthur does not support this teaching, but I do because I am not a five-point Calvinist. My "age of accountability" teaching starts when the child knows already how to believe in Jesus. Observe John 3:36: "He who believes in the Son has eternal life." One Christian blogger also suggested that Isaiah 7 seems to suggest accountability when it says, "the boy will know enough to refuse evil and choose good." (Vv. 15-16)

Once a person understands his need for salvation and the urgency attached to it, he would listen to the word of God.

My spiritual wirings seem to connect for me to figure out I had a problem with God as I struggled to understand death—the death of a loved one! I got so motivated to know more about life after death, and the Holy Spirit worked with me through the grace of God and gave me spiritual awareness. I was like a dead computer that flickered the screen and hinted at a little sign of life, for my heart struggled to comprehend the grave. Reads Romans 1:19 that what "is known about God is evident within them; for God made it evident to them." Searching for the spiritual side of life had just become my passion as my mind craved for the truth about the untimely death of my father. And God was there helping me in my quest to understand it. He used a pastor who was my classmate in a master's course to share with me Hebrews 9:27, where it says death is an appointment. This Bible message satisfied my soul like meds, healing my pains. Attending a Christian church for the first time, I learned I had sinned against God; that I am not worthy of God's attention, since He is holy and hates sinners, His enemies! Then the preacher preached the Gospel; he preached the love of Jesus!

My conversion process, as I listened, got sweetened by the Word of God and initialized like dry yeast bubbling for a new life. I learned of my sinfulness against my Creator, but the Son of God, Jesus Christ, rescued me and paid for all my transgressions by His own blood. Then the pastor read Psalm 103, where my faith and love for Jesus reached a decisive moment. He started in verse 9 and ended in verse 14:

He will not always strive with us,
Nor will He keep His anger forever.
He has not dealt with us according to our sins,
Nor rewarded us according to our iniquities.
For as high as the heavens are above the earth,
So great is His lovingkindness toward those who fear Him.
As far as the east is from the west,
far has He removed our transgressions from us.
Just as a father has compassion on his children,
So the Lord has compassion on those who fear Him.
For He Himself knows our frame;
He is mindful that we are but dust.

Had I not trusted the Bible as the very Word of God, what would have been my response when the psalmist said, "As far as the east is from the west, far has He removed our transgressions from us"?

I would not have appreciated the grace of God. But I trusted the Scriptures, my only source for truth. Christ gave me forgiveness through His sacrificial death on the cross as an offering for my sin. And that pardon covers all my sins. Said Paul: So "that you are not lacking in any gift, awaiting eagerly the revelation of our Lord Jesus Christ, who will also confirm you to the end, BLAMELESS IN THE DAY OF OUR LORD JESUS CHRIST. God is faithful, through whom you were called into fellowship with His Son, Jesus Christ our Lord." (1 Cor. 1:7-9)

Born again means salvation; our soul's salvation from God's wrath and judgment, given the fact of our sinfulness and hardness of heart to believe.

Born Again is a Conviction that Salvation is Free

God provided us salvation and eternal life for free. What to do to be born again? Nothing—except to trust Jesus as Lord, Savior, and God the Son. The Father gave us our first birth for free, just as He made the second-birth experience free for those who accept and trust Christ.

We are all sinners but are saved for free, according to Romans 3. For "all have sinned and fall short of the glory of God, being justified [or made righteous] as a gift by His grace through the redemption which is in Christ Jesus." Our justification or righteousness is a gift by His grace through Christ's redemptive work.

In Ephesians 2:8-9, Paul said, "For by grace you have been saved through faith; and that not of yourselves, it is the gift of God; not as a result of works, so that no one may boast."

We can't help loving this Scripture just quoted. The second birth is God's gift because eternal life is God's grace. This Gift is Christ Himself. For God gave His only begotten Son to ransom us from the slave market of sin.

Before writing that salvation (or the born-again experience) is the gift of God and is, therefore, given to us for free, Paul wrote that

"But God, being rich in mercy, because of His great love with which He loved us, even when we were dead in our transgressions, made us alive together with Christ (by grace you have been saved), and raised us up with Him, and seated us with Him in the heavenly places in Christ Jesus, so that in the ages to come He might show the surpassing riches of His grace in kindness toward us in Christ Jesus." (Eph. 2:4-7)

From this Scripture, we learned our God's desire to "show the surpassing riches of His grace in kindness toward us in Christ Jesus." Let's observe two things here. One is God's love or grace toward us, and two, His condition to nail this love only in Christ Jesus.

But what is God's grace? It is His favor to those who don't deserve His blessing. We don't deserve Christ's atoning blood, but God sacrificed His own beloved Son, Jesus, to provide satisfaction and atonement for our sins. "For God so loved the world that He gave His only begotten Son, that whoever believes in Him shall not perish, but have eternal life." God gave Jesus to redeem us from sin. Christ is the Father's unsurpassed love, His undeserved kindness.

If you trust Jesus—like you'll never recant even amid the ISIS-style of terror evangelism! — then you will have eternal life. You are born again, not because of your righteousnesses but because you believe in Jesus like you believe you can't speak without your tongue or you can't walk without your feet.

Salvation is free, but you need to believe, trust, and rely upon Jesus.

The Christian Church got its footing from the born-again Christian's version of faith in the finished work of Jesus at

Calvary. And the Holy Spirit's watch over the Church and His witness through the Scriptures and the affirmation of the Christian martyrs' blood nursed her growth for over two thousand years.

Faith in Jesus, therefore, which saves a soul is not just your mere promise to trust Him but your commitment to die for your Christian conviction.

Time will come when governments would forcibly microchip all citizens, or they cannot buy things, according to the Bible. (Cf. Rev. 13:17) Microchip insertion could be the acid test for our faith in Christ soon. Few companies are now microchipping their employees. Our tribulation as born-again Christians is in the wind.

After teaching that self-righteousness would only lead to boasting (Eph. 2:9) Paul required us, born-again Christians, to do good deeds in verse ten: "For we are His workmanship, created in Christ Jesus for good works, which God prepared beforehand so that we would walk in them." (Eph. 2:10)

The Christian's love for the lost, for example, comes out of the second birth experience. Salvation is free, hence it is not biblical to say that our charities and righteous deeds may influence God to grant us salvation and eternal life. We cannot buy forgiveness with our self-righteousness—we cannot bribe God! Now, we have a question: Why are born-again Christians doing good deeds? The answer is that we are God's "workmanship, created in Christ Jesus for good works."

Self-sufficiency is Paul's description of good works, aside from his extremely perilous ministry of planting the Lord's churches. He also said you are worse than the unbeliever if you claim Christianity but won't provide for your own family. (Cf. 1 Tim. 5:8) It is better to offer help than to wait for someone in decades to help you.

In Acts 20, Paul said:

"I have coveted no one's silver or gold or clothes. You yourselves know that these hands ministered to my own needs and to the men who were with me. In everything I showed you that by working hard in this manner you must help the weak and remember the words of the Lord Jesus, that He Himself said, 'It is more blessed to give than to receive.'" (Acts 20:33-35)

The freeness of salvation entails the freeness of good deeds the born-again Christians may offer naturally to those in need.

Born Again is a Union with Christ

I talked with someone who became a pastor later in his life. For his second birth experience, he told me he spoke in tongues before he knew and received the Lord Jesus in his heart. Later in his ministry, we heard he had issues with a guy who called him "pastor" sarcastically. He lost patience, according to witnesses, and collared a former friend who poked fun at him. The story did not end there, as he got involved with many other controversies.

Born again signifies our union with Christ's Spirit. Hence, a Christian who steps out of line may have sprung up from those faking their born-again experience. Paul said: "But the one who joins himself to the Lord is one spirit with Him." (1 Cor. 6:17)

The Liberals and pseudo-Christians have one thing in common, which is a fake second birth experience. Paul said, "if anyone is in Christ." It is the start of the scriptural (or we may say legitimate) born-again experience. You are in Christ Jesus by faith. If your strange emotions during a worship event had made you babble with strange words flowing out of your mouth even before knowing Christ, it could be a miracle of tongues, but not from God's Spirit. If you allegedly speak in tongues before meeting Christ by faith, it could be a sign, alright, but not from God! Haven't you performed signs and wonders by the aid of the devil's deceitful spirits? Christianity is contact with Christ by faith. Performing a speaking in tongues scene even before a born again event is just anomalous if not demonic!

I experienced being filled with God's Spirit as I delivered a sermon one Sunday morning. My message was a simple evangelistic exhortation, but few visitors received our Lord and they cried silently. I noticed them and got overjoyed for a handful of saved souls. I felt the love of God embracing my spirit, but I kept my emotions down while thanking our Lord for using me. The love of God always defines my union with Christ. This is how Paul describes his unity with Christ: The "love of God has been poured out within our hearts through the Holy Spirit who was given to us." (Rom. 5:5)

The born-again reality is a relationship with Christ, where stories of the Holy Spirit's saving a soul are splendid news. "In the same way, I tell you," said Christ, "there is joy in the presence of the angels of God over one sinner who repents." (Luke 15:10)

Can we imagine the joy in heaven as the angels of God celebrate for one soul who repented and got saved? Our union with Christ through the born-again experience is just something very close to the heart of our Father God.

Born Again Means Christ's Exaltation

Our Father God exalted Christ highly and "bestowed on Him the name which is above every name, so that at the name of Jesus every knee will bow, of those who are in heaven and on earth and under the earth, and that every tongue will confess that Jesus Christ is Lord, to the glory of God the Father." (Phil.

2:9-11) The Father is glorified when Christ gets exalted.

The common trait of those not born of God is their giving glory and more regard to the local church of their membership, to the leaders, and the fellowship. It is not wrong to give an excessive interest in everything related to the Assembly. It is not improper to have a super love for the church. Paul said, "Husbands, love your wives, just as Christ also loved the church and gave Himself up for her." (Eph. 5:25) We need to love and support the church. Where will our children go without our church?

The born-again Christian, however, loves and exalts Christ the way incomparable with his devotion to his fellowship. He is Christ-centered, like a compass always pointing to the North Pole. When there's a sermon, he would look for his Lord's glory, and when there's a church meeting or event, he would expect the honored place of Jesus in it.

When the local church's leadership adapts Liberalism, the born-again Christian will be the first one to object.

I attended a worship service where one old woman wore earplugs to endure the pentecostalized noise her Baptist church adapted.

Who is glorified when you speak in tongues, which is no better than babbling in contrast with the biblical tongues? (See Acts 2:5-15)

Who is glorified when the church rebrands pop and rock songs to "praise and worship" music and then makes the congregants spectators of the concert-like worship event?

For the born-again Christian, everything church-related must redound immensely to the honor and exaltation of Jesus.

In most Baptist and non-Pentecostal denominations of the religious divide, the churchgoers tend to find a Church

Solidarity or Sisterhood Club in the church. No one is excited about the sermon or the Sunday school. Everybody is looking forward to meeting their church friends. Church attendance becomes a habit with zero retention for the word of God (except for the pastor's stories and jokes!) after the worship service.

Our churches have become powerless.

Here is Dr. John R. Rice's observation:

"The first need of Christians today is not training. We have brains, the culture, the personality in the pulpits of our land. But sinners do not tremble and repent. Saints do not fall in confession and holy rededication before God. Drunkards are not made sober. Harlots are not made pure. Infidels are not made believers. It is not training but power that we lack and need . . . Most of our preaching, most of our singing, most of our testimony, most of our praying, most of our living is without power. We do not have the breath of God upon us. Heaven is shut up so that there is little spiritual rain. God has turned His face away from us! Oh, the crying shame and sin and defeat and ruin and death of our powerless lives!"[22]

How to debug this Laodicean (or lukewarm) shift of the churches? Well, born-again Christianity, which pursues Christ's exaltation at every turn.

Born Again is an Encounter with Christ

We know there's always love in a Christian assembly, but an excellent church fellowship cannot save you from hell. First, we need to meet the Lord Jesus by faith, not just the church. It is the essence of the second birth event in life. It is an

---

[22] John R. Rice, The Power of Pentecost or Fullness of the Spirit (Tennessee: Sword of the Lord Publishers, 1949), p. 17.

encounter with the risen Jesus spiritually!

We had a Sunday school teacher who was an active member as a deacon and choir guy. He met with one crisis after the other, from economic to health issues. Later, he testified he didn't have a prayer life. A non-praying deacon is just suspect for a Christless guy enjoying the pedestal of the church leadership.

That is why Christ taught Nicodemus about born again or spiritual transformation as the only ticket to enter heaven to erase any stamp of confusion and false doctrine. Folks, it is not church membership or deep involvement in church activities. It is not speaking in tongues or the ability to implore signs and wonders. Born again is an encounter with Christ.

One man also told me he's born again because he's so happy with his church activities. Wasn't Judas also happy with his fellowship with Christ's disciples, whom he worked with for three consecutive years? The second birth is an experience of salvation as promised that you "may know that you have eternal life." (1 John 5:13) It is union with the risen Christ's Spirit, and it has nothing to do with a Christian camaraderie.

An encounter with Christ is a definite experience. "Zacchaeus," Christ called him out, "hurry and come down, for today I must stay at your house." (Luke 19:5) Up in a sycamore tree hugging a branch, this little man experienced hearing Christ's speaking to him and calling him by his name. Then, Christ also promised to stay in his house. The Bible said Zacchaeus was small in stature, so he climbed up into a sycamore tree to have a full view of Jesus who was passing by Jericho. Jesus acknowledged his faith and saved him, and the Holy Spirit sealed up Zacchaeus and stayed in his house, which is his body, the temple of God's Spirit. The second birth is the Spirit's indwelling, and it would happen to anyone meeting Christ and trusting His name. Yes, an encounter with

Christ is a positive experience with His Spirit who is also the Spirit of God.

I read somewhere about a guy who was a drug addict and committing crimes on a daily basis. The prison cell becomes his home. Desperate after a 25-year term in jail, he opened the Bible and from there he met Christ. He said, "For the first time I opened a Bible, and the Lord spoke to me in Jeremiah 33:3. As I started to read the Bible I couldn't stop crying and I fell in love with Jesus. I was facing 25 to life and yet the Lord had set me free. I was released after serving 17 months."

Born again is an encounter with Christ.

Born Again is Divine Forgiveness

Before I became a born-again Christian, success books and political issues captivated me. I never studied Jesus, heaven, and the other eternal things enshrined in the Holy Scriptures. For around 27 years of life, I never had an interest in God. I missed God in my life's computer screen if life were a list of menu options. Material success preoccupied all my waking hours until my conversion. The apostle Paul penned the doctrinal threshold of my experience along these lines: "For He rescued us from the domain of darkness, and transferred us to the kingdom of His beloved Son, in whom we have redemption, the forgiveness of sins." (Col. 1:13-14) My life's U-turn from a 24/7 material man to a follower of Jesus happened after I received the forgiveness of my sins through faith in Christ—after my Lord redeemed my soul from the powers of darkness. Paul defines redemption (or salvation) as "the forgiveness of sins." He also said that before my divine forgiveness I lived in the "domain of darkness." This Scripture in Colossians chapter one just provided unbroken muscles for the skeletal sketch of my born again story.

The second birth is experiential. You cannot experience it

by a mere head knowledge of the doctrine.

When Paul said God rescued me from the domain of darkness, I knew it and could explain it, too!

Concerning divine forgiveness, which describes further the second birth experience, Christ said we can sense its work inside of us spiritually. After receiving your wife's forgiveness, for example, you would have peace with her, which produces a fountain of joy in your heart.

Observe Christ's word to Nicodemus in John 3:7-8: "Do not be amazed that I said to you, 'You must be born again.' The wind blows where it wishes and you hear the sound of it, but do not know where it comes from and where it is going; so is everyone who is born of the Spirit." We can experience the cool breeze touching our checks, right? Christ said you hear the wind howls and sighs. Thus, the born-again experience is brought down to the carnal senses from its spiritual dawning. With it, you can always know your eternal life as taught by John (See 1 John 5:13). Hence, your assurance of eternal salvation is not just a pure biblical theory!

Second, the second birth is just like the mystery of the wind because it is mysterious (from the Holy Spirit) and not the product of man's efforts.

How do we connect divine forgiveness with the born again phenomenon?"

We wrote somewhere in this book that our sins have separated us from our Creator. Adam and Eve's escape from Paradise illustrates this truth. Judas also left Christ's fellowship after betraying our Lord.

Our sins against God must have a perfect ransom or deliverance to qualify us for immortality in heaven. We need God's forgiveness. Our Lord Jesus condescended to offer His own blood on the cross. Paul validated this divine plan by saying, "In Him we have redemption through His blood, the forgiveness of our trespasses, according to the riches of His grace which He lavished on us." (Eph. 1:7-8)

To sum up this teaching, Christ said that the Father in heaven gave His Son, Jesus, as man's Redeemer through our faith in His shed blood at Calvary. The apostle Paul spoke for this position when he said, "This is good and acceptable in the sight of God our Savior, who desires all men to be saved and to come to the knowledge of the truth. For there is one God, and one mediator also between God and men, the man Christ Jesus, who gave Himself as a ransom for all." Christ is our Mediator and Redeemer. His sacred blood on the cross washes away our sins if we will give to Him our heart by faith and complete trust.

Divine forgiveness is just the umbilical cord of the second birth. And Christ owns every nook and cranny of divine clemency. Observe Luke 5:20: "Seeing their faith, He said, 'Friend, your sins are forgiven you.'" (Luke 5:20) Two words make emphatic this verse. They are "faith" and "forgiven." In short, our faith in Christ's atoning blood guarantees our redemption. Wrote the apostle Peter: "The reward for trusting him will be the salvation of your souls." (1 Pet. 1:9, NLT)

Someone said his sins were just venial as he had not killed a person; he had stolen nothing. He didn't need Jesus to ransom his soul. But the most horrifying sin is neither stealing nor killing, but rejecting Jesus. Christ said, "he who does not believe has been judged already." (John 3:18) It means if you had rejected Jesus at age 20, then you were judged by God from that time onward. At age 40, you had stockpiled God's wrath on your person already for the past twenty years. You may have a failed marriage, a serious health problem, or a boring job since the wrath of God abides on him who rejects Jesus. (John 3:36)

In Colossians 1:17, Paul said Christ "is before all things, and in Him all things hold together." He is before all things because He is God the Son. If Christ turns His back on you, then all things would work together to bring you down. Have you heard of successful people living miserable lives? It is the point. Peace is the greatest source of joy in life, and this Peace is Christ Himself. He is the owner of divine peace. He said, "Peace I leave with you; My peace I give to you; not as the world gives do I give to you." (John 14:27) You may have just constructed your fourth mansion, and inaugurated your new five-star hotel, but without the hope of God and His promised eternal life in Christ, your life would simply be a lust after the wind. This explains why billionaires Henry Sy, Jr. (Philippines) and Philip Ng (Singapore) followed Jesus. Ng even testified that the "missing piece was God through Jesus Christ" in his billionaire life.

Of the unbelieving rich man, Christ said through a parable: "'You fool! This very night your soul is required of you; and now who will own what you have prepared?' So is the man who stores up treasure for himself, and is not rich toward God." (Luke 12:20-21)

"After all," wrote Paul, "we brought nothing with us when we came into the world, and we can't take anything with us when we leave it." (1 Tim. 6:7, NLT)

Yes, born again is divine forgiveness. And only Christ can offer complete forgiveness to your soul as what He did with Mary Magdalene or the repentant thief on the cross. Wrote Paul: "In Him [Christ] we have redemption through His blood, the forgiveness of our trespasses, according to the riches of His grace which He lavished on us." (Eph. 1:7-8a) And from the Book of Hebrews, chapter 10, the Bible said:

"By this will we have been sanctified through the offering of the body of Jesus Christ once for all. For by one offering He has perfected for all time those who are sanctified. And the Holy Spirit also testifies to us; for after saying . . . 'And their sins and their lawless deeds. I will remember no more.' Now where there is forgiveness of these things, there is no longer any offering for sin." (Heb. 10:10, 14-18)

Christ's divine forgiveness is perfect; hence we wrote somewhere that once a person is born of God, he is forgiven and saved, and heaven is his home after this life.

A person who is not born again does not possess such faith, assurance, and hope of eternal bliss.

8. NO LONGER A PHENOMENON

Jesus answered and said to him, "Truly, truly, I say to you, unless one is born again he cannot see the kingdom of God." — John 3:3.

THE BORN-AGAIN EXPERIENCE is a phenomenon since it is a fact that is observable, but people impugned its cause or explanation. For the Bible believers, however, this experience is caused by God through His Spirit, and not just a mere phenomenon. Science preaches hypothesis as a limited explanation of a phenomenon; a theory as its in-depth explanation; and a law (like the Law of Gravity) as a unifying statement about an observed phenomenon.

The Liberals applaud the scientific concept of bringing up the truth of anything through repeated and observable experiments. They support REASON as superior and preferable over FAITH. Since they cannot put God, Jesus Christ, the Holy Spirit, or life after death into their experiment lab, their best option is to declare that God is dead, and the Bible is a myth.

As they cannot make the Bible truths experimental subjects, so they failed their academic scrutiny of them. Their position about religious wars and bigotry has justified their hatred toward the Scriptures. One of them, Ruth Hurmence Green, expressed well this thought by saying, "There was a time when religion ruled the world. It is known as the Dark Ages."

How can they uncover the truth about the virgin birth of Christ or His resurrection, for example, by mere scientific experiments or through the eye of a thousand philosophical paradigms? For this instance, A. W. Tozer said FAITH is superior to REASON. He wrote:

"Reason could not tell us that Jesus Christ should be born of a virgin, but faith knows that He was . . .

"Reason cannot say, 'I know that He will come to judge the quick and the dead,' but faith knows that He will come. Reason cannot say, 'My sins are all gone,' but faith knows that they are forgiven and forgotten."[23]

Jesus Christ said we must be born again. Whatever that means, we need to understand and experience it to enter heaven and "see the kingdom of God." The Liberals want to use their mind tools and a thousand philosophies to chew over the Word of God by the teeth of their finite brains. But God said your faith should not "rest on the wisdom of men, but on the power of God." He didn't say "your research," but "your faith." (1 Cor. 2:5)

From most of my readings about the "God is dead" subject flooding the Internet, I realized the homosexual issues got the central thesis. These scholarly atheists hate Christianity so much because God said He would soon burn the unrepentant gays as He did with Sodom and Gomorrah.

The word "born again" means "born of God" or "born of the Spirit of God." It will happen when one accepts the claims of Christ as the Lord and Savior of humanity from sin. Nicodemus got confused about this teaching since it is impossible to return to mother's womb, he said, and be born the second time. But Christ told him that the first birth is "of the flesh," the second is by the Spirit.

---

[23] A. W. Tozer, The Tozer Pulpit, Volume One, Book 3, Chapter 3 (Christian Publications, Camp Hill, PA 17011, 1994), pp. 48-49; 51.

No Longer a Phenomenon: Born Again is the Indwelling of the Holy Spirit

The second birth requirement to get salvation and be with God in heaven consists in the indwelling of the Holy Spirit. The apostle Paul made it indisputable in Romans 8:11, when he says, "But if the Spirit of Him who raised Jesus from the dead DWELLS IN YOU, He who raised Christ Jesus from the dead will also give life to your mortal bodies through His Spirit who DWELLS IN YOU." (Rom. 8:11)

You will experience the second birth when the Holy Spirit lives in your body as you believe and trust in Christ and His promises.

Paul explained further this doctrine on how to be born again in Galatians chapter three, where he asked: "Are you so foolish? Having begun by the Spirit, are you now being perfected by the flesh? So then, does He who provides you with the Spirit and works miracles among you, do it by the works of the Law, or by hearing with faith?" (Gal. 3:3, 5) In effect, the Apostle taught it is sheer foolishness to get the second birth seal from God based on good works like baptism, involvement with church activities, or doing good deeds to your neighbors. For we can be born again only through genuine faith in Christ and when the Holy Spirit indwells us — "since the flesh cannot perfect us."

We had a friend, an active member of the Seventh Day Adventist group. All our chats about religion recoil to her charities and self-righteousness. She was praising herself indirectly though because of her goodwill and generosity. But then comes her great trial, and she didn't know where to go for help. We told her to pray but asked us instead to pray for her. She does not know where, how, and when to pray to Jesus because she didn't have the Spirit of Christ (See Rom. 8:9).

She was not born of the Spirit of God. A zealot-SDA, she had never been born again. The Holy Spirit did not live in her soul.

No Longer a Phenomenon: Born Again is God's Intervention in the Second Birth Process

The second birth is a miracle if we believe that a miracle is the suspension of the natural law. The term "natural law" is awkward in the scope of our discussion, but we want to stress a point here. First, why is it that a three-year-old child already tells big lies without any tutorial lessons from the School of Liars? When asked why her Dad and Mom had a heated discussion, my three-year-old granddaughter said, "No." She lied, of course. Then, a follow-up question: "Why the heated discussion?" "Secret," she replied. Applying the natural-law or natural-propensity concept we find that we are born in sin. To sin is instinctive and a big player in our inborn traits.

Paul said we are all sinners (Rom. 6:23), and David pushed further the teaching by saying that "in sin my mother conceived me." (Ps. 51:5) We "speak lies and go astray from birth," according to Psalm 58:3. We were "a rebel from birth," wrote the prophet Isaiah. (Is. 48:8) That said, it takes a miracle to live a 360-degree regenerated life in Christ Jesus. That is why Christ taught that "apart from Me you can do nothing." (John 15:5) The second birth is a miracle of newness, from the harlot Magdalene to Saint Magdalene — from the unbelieving Thomas to the new, born-again Thomas.

Without this supernatural occurrence in the soul that happened with the born-again experience, then we could be a member of the church like the unsaved Judas, who was a fake Christian. To be born again is to be saved, and to be saved is possible only with Christ's intervention. Observed Matthew 19:25-26: "When the disciples heard this, they were very astonished and said, 'Then who can be saved?' And looking at them Jesus said to them, 'With people this is impossible, but with God all things are possible.'"

The second birth is experienced by all born-again Christians the world over. They have the same Holy Spirit and similar testimonials about Christ's love and power to answer prayers.

We can tell if the preacher or Sunday school teacher is not born again since "the flesh sets its desire against the Spirit . . . these are in opposition to one another." (Gal. 5:17) Your Spirit opposes the demons, tenanting the rejecters of Christ.

The Father in heaven "rescued us from the domain of darkness, and transferred us to the kingdom of His beloved Son, in whom we have redemption, the forgiveness of sins." (Col. 2:13-14)

In short, it's a big deal—we are different; we are the people of God! The second birth is a definite experience. The unbelievers laugh at it and invent all sorts of scornful adjectives to describe it. Some even call the born-again phenomenon "born against" or similar empty sarcasm. But they just missed the point of Christ, namely, that the second birth is the gauge of true Christianity.

If you are born just once, then you cannot see heaven and the kingdom of God—even if you have a physical membership with the Lord's Church. Your portion is hell and you better rack your brains on that.

We need the second birth because Christ said so. And the doctrine is that when He gives the requirement to be born again, He would also give us the ability to comply and obey what He required us to do. His order is for us to believe in Him, and it is not rocket science. You don't need to attend a church, listen to a sermon, or attend a seminary training to believe. You can do it right now, isn't it? Invite His Spirit into your heart, and He will take care of the rest in the second birth event.

Speaking of faith, here is Christ's Word: "As Moses lifted up the serpent in the wilderness, even so must the Son of Man be lifted up; so that whoever **believes** will in Him have eternal life. For God so loved the world, that He gave His only begotten Son, that whoever **believes** in Him shall not perish, but have eternal life." (John 3:14-16)

Believing in Christ is not rocket engineering. Even a mere child can do it! The Holy Spirit will take care of the other elements of the second birth. Repentance, for example, is required, too. But, no worries, it is a part of faith. And the Holy Spirit will teach you repentance. In my experience, no one lectured me about repentance. If you believe you are hypertensive, for example, you will change your lifestyle. A friend told me his doctor required him to undergo heart surgery. He died after few months after he rejected his doctor's advice. If you believe in Christ, you will turn to God and leave your sinful life. "Now repent of your sins and turn to God." (Acts 3:19b, NLT)

Here is one relevant statement concerning the faith-and-repentance connection:

"Regeneration, or the new birth, is a work of God's grace whereby believers become new creatures in Christ Jesus. It is a change of heart wrought by the Holy Spirit through conviction of sin, to which the sinner responds in repentance toward God and faith in the Lord Jesus Christ. Repentance and faith are inseparable experiences of grace. Repentance is a genuine turning from sin toward God. Faith is the acceptance of Jesus Christ and commitment of the entire personality to Him as Lord and Saviour."[24]

No Longer a Phenomenon: Born Again is the Other Half of Man's Dual Nature

A person who has the Spirit of God assumes a dual nature. The internet roars in the mere mention of the dual nature theory. But it is the truth. Sometimes we are spiritual, sometimes not. John Wesley preached sinless perfection and lived what he taught. Later in life, he said he's far from perfect. Wrote the apostle John that "If we say that we have no sin, we are deceiving ourselves and the truth is not in us." (1 John 1:8) A sinless perfection in this life is not possible. The difference is that the believers of Christ are no longer a slave to sin. A homosexual who will be converted to Christianity, for example, will leave his old life as the Holy Spirit will teach him the Word of God. That is the bottom line of true conversion. But he continues to sin occasionally since "everyone who looks at a woman with lust for her has already committed adultery with her in his heart." (Matt. 5:28) God's Law is perfect; we are not. Second, the apostle Paul lectured to the brethren at Corinth that he "could not speak to [them] as to spiritual men, but as to men of flesh, as to infants in Christ." (1 Cor. 3:1) The dual nature is mentioned here as the "spiritual men" and the "men of the flesh" or carnal Christians. Again, the difference is that the born-again believers of Jesus do not maintain a sinful life. Observe this teaching from John: "If we say that we have fellowship with Him [Christ] and yet walk in the darkness, we lie and do not practice the truth." (1 John 1:6) Indeed, we are victorious over the power of sin as genuine

---

[24] Livingstone, Mike. "THE REPENTANCE-FAITH CONNECTION (SESSION 12 — ACTS 26:19-29)". goexplorethebible.com. https://goexplorethebible.com/blog/adults/the-repentance-faith-connection-session-12-acts-2619-29/ (accessed November 29, 2020).

believers. If you have two wives before and after your conversion, to use the apostle Paul: "Test yourselves to see if you are in the faith; examine yourselves! Or do you not recognize this about yourselves that Jesus Christ is in you—unless indeed you fail the test?" (2 Cor. 13:5) Born-again Christians do not live in sin. Having two wives is proof of slavery to sin. It is fake Christianity in its fullness.

The Conflict of Two Natures

The New American Standard Bible has this caption in Romans 6:14-25: "The Conflict of Two Natures." I want to share verses 14-20 of it, to show furthermore the scripturalness of the dual-nature teaching:

> For we know that the Law is spiritual, but I am of flesh, sold into bondage to sin. For what I am doing, I do not understand; for I am not practicing what I would like to do, but I am doing the very thing I hate. But if I do the very thing I do not want to do, I agree with the Law, confessing that the Law is good. So now, no longer am I the one doing it, but sin which dwells in me. For I know that nothing good dwells in me, that is, in my flesh; for the willing is present in me, but the doing of the good is not. For the good that I want, I do not do, but I practice the very evil that I do not want. But if I am doing the very thing I do not want, I am no longer the one doing it, but sin which dwells in me.

The born-again experience is not sinless perfection. Wrote one church leader who left the faith: "Christians can be the most judgmental people on the planet." Those not born of God see the light upon Christ's followers as judgmentalism, seeing their imperfections. Christ has clarified this judgmentalism-issue roaring in Facebook. "This is the judgment, that the Light has come into the world, and men loved the darkness rather than the Light, for their deeds were evil." (John 3:19) If you are a fake Christian like the former Hillsong songwriter, you would say you're being judged by your church. But it is required as a believer (unless you're a fake!). The first requirement is to examine yourself if you are in the faith as we mentioned earlier. Examine yourself if Jesus is in you. (Cf. 2 Cor. 13:5) If Christ is not in you, you will fail the test and leave Christianity and say all things negative about the people of God, the born-again Christians. And the second precondition is for the church to judge you. Said Paul: "For what have I to do with judging outsiders? Do you not judge those who are within the church? But those who are outside, God judges. Remove the wicked man from among yourselves." (1 Cor. 5:12-13) Those church leaders leaving Christianity left because they don't meet God's standard, which is to experience the second birth to be saved.

Without Christ's Spirit in your soul, your church membership is like the case of a blind man describing colors, to use Spurgeon's description of the unsaved. It is torturous to flock together with birds of different feathers.

The born-again Christian is not perfect, but he is different; he is a follower of Jesus—a disciple of the Light of this world!

No Longer a Phenomenon: Born Again Means a Changed Life

I taught the Gospel to someone who was an alcoholic and a very irresponsible family man. Later, he testified that his previous church failed to lead him to salvation through real faith in Jesus. In short, he was a fake guy before he finally became a genuine Christian. He always had a bottle of liquor anywhere he went. Then, we all saw his 360-degree change from a drunken father to an active church leader. "There is victory in Jesus," goes a hymn. It is true. Paul said that "God . . . always leads us in triumph in Christ." How sin is powerless in our lives?

The apostle Paul taught in Romans chapter 6 that a born-again person is positionally dead to sin because, in principle, he was crucified with Christ. Paul made it unmistakable in Galatians 2:20. "I have been crucified with Christ," he said, "and it is no longer I who live, but Christ lives in me." A real Christian is not a slave to sin.

If you're a "Christian" but without a victory over sin, then you are not born again according to the Word of God. I have friends who told me I was judging, for which I reminded them to check the Bible and steer clear of opinions. Wrote Paul: "Do not be deceived; neither fornicators . . . nor effeminate, nor homosexuals . . . will inherit the kingdom of God." (1 Cor. 6:9b-10) An LGBT Christian is not a Christian at all because a genuine believer is victorious over sin. We heard about lesbian pastors; God's Word does not teach that!

I find from the internet a former gay's statement after his conversion: "It became clear to me," he said, ". . . that homosexuality prevents us from finding our true self within. We cannot see the truth when we're blinded by homosexuality."

The pressure from the unbelievers (the LGBT communities included) is for Christians to present the love of Christ and not the judgment of God. What scares the immoral people inside the church is the members' judgmentalism. It is echoing Mahatma Gandhi's observation: "I like your Christ, I do not like your Christians. Your Christians are so unlike your Christ."

The love of the Christians to the unbelievers helped a lot. I experienced it before I became a believer. Missions involving tons of money took root because of this love. But I don't believe that the life of sin (homosexuality, robbery, prostitution, etc.) should be tolerated because the Bible required us to "abstain from every form of evil." (1 Thess. 5:22) "Therefore if you have been raised up with Christ, keep seeking the things above, where Christ is . . . Set your mind on the things above, not on the things that are on earth." (Col. 3:1-2) The Liberal churches are all love and accommodation, but it is not Bible Christianity. Preach sin, even if it hurts those in the pews, for God is not just love. He's also a sin-hater and a judge. To the woman caught in adultery, Christ said: "sin no more."

No Longer a Phenomenon: Born Again Leads to the Christian's Spirit-controlled Life

The pseudo-Christians continue with the pursuits of their old sinful selves, having no victory over the shameful lusts of this world. On TV, and even on some Facebook posts, we find women who discuss God or share Bible verses while wearing tight, breast-accentuated objectionable clothing. Taught the apostle Paul: "Put to death therefore what is earthly in you: sexual immorality, impurity, passion, evil desire, and covetousness, which is idolatry. On account of these, the wrath of God is coming." The fake Christians can never hide their affection for everything obnoxious before God in this life. But we, born-again Christians, are different. For we have a victory over this world's orgies and evil culture because of the grace and mercy of Christ to His own beloved and chosen people, the Spirit-controlled Christians.

In Romans chapter 6, Paul taught that,

"Now if we have died with Christ, we believe that we shall also live with Him, knowing that Christ, having been raised from the dead, is never to die again; death no longer is master over Him. For the death that He died, He died to sin once for all; but the life that He lives, He lives to God. Even so consider yourselves to be dead to sin, but alive to God in Christ Jesus."

(Rom. 6:8-11)

No Longer a Phenomenon: Born Again Gives One Life's Victory through Christ's Intercession

I saw a post on Facebook about a letter from a 15-year-old girl before she committed suicide. The first part of her message to her parents focuses on her sense of emptiness and hunger for love despite her folks' abundant provisions. Then, her uncle's sexual abuses, and lastly, her pastor's "long sermons." This incident explains the inner chaos of a person attending church but does not have the victory over the rule of sin. It is a story of a fake Christian struggling and beaten by the force of her transgressions and guilt complex. The born-again Christian will never commit suicide in the same array of circumstances, given Christ's love and intervention. "No temptation has overtaken you," taught the apostle Paul, "but such as is common to man; and God is faithful, who will not allow you to be tempted beyond what you are able, but with the temptation will provide the way of escape also, so that you will be able to endure it." (1 Cor. 10:13)

We can defeat sin because of Christ's intercession.

The young girl we mentioned above killed herself out of confusion, guilt, and a sense of emptiness because of sin and rejection of God's Word. She tolerated her uncle (did not inform her mother of the sexual assaults) and disliked long sermons.

The born-again mind will never commit suicide because the Spirit of God in the soul won't allow it. The Word of God is the sword of the Spirit (Eph. 6:17), and we can use it to ensure victory against the enemy, who is the devil. Second, "Christ Jesus is He who died, yes, rather who was raised, who is at the right hand of God, who also intercedes for us." (Rom. 8:34) Christ Himself will plead for us!

No Longer a Phenomenon: Born Again Produces Life's Newness

The born-again person is born of God's Spirit. In Romans 8:9, Christ's Spirit indwells the believer, and the result is the newness of life. What is this newness? Many debated on this teaching because of the depth of Paul's statement: "he is a new creature; the old things passed away; behold, new things have come." (2 Cor. 5:17) This "newness" is equivalent to a "new creature" — the old things passed away! When I received Christ over three decades ago, my physical body did not "passed away." So, the new creature description is not the physical person. When Paul got converted, he was the same person except for his new name and radical U-turn from a persecutor to an apostle of Jesus. This newness, therefore, exists in the mind, the heart, and soul of the believer. As such, the born-again Christian got a brand-new life he was ignorant about before experiencing the Christ-attuned thoughts and desires of the saved soul. The prophet Ezekiel also wrote about this newness of life:

> "Moreover, I will give you a new heart and put a new spirit within you; and I will remove the heart of stone from your flesh and give you a heart of flesh." (Ezek. 36:26)

The owners of "Walmart," "Hobby Lobby," "Forever 21," not to mention the others, are Bible believers who have proven a lifestyle and faith different from the typical wealthy individuals. A newness in Christ is a reality and not just a bare phenomenon.

Said C. H. Spurgeon: "Another proof of the conquest of a soul for Christ will be found in a real change of life. If the man does not live differently from what he did before, both at home and abroad, his repentance needs repented of, and his conversion is a fiction. "

No Longer a Phenomenon: Born Again Leads One to Experience Christian Peace

One trait of a genuine Christian is the desire to live in peace and to be at peace with everybody. When there is a controversy, he is the first one to suggest a truce for the pacification of everyone. Paul said, "If possible, so far as it depends on you, be at peace with all men." (Rom. 12:18) The Christian's favorite verse is John 14:27 which says that Christ will give to His follower His very own divine peace. What will happen to the soul ruled by Christ's peace? Observe this teaching of our Lord:

> "Peace I leave with you; My peace I give to you; not as the world gives do I give to you. Do not let your heart be troubled, nor let it be fearful."

This peace package rises above the level of the familiar serenity we experienced in this world. If this trait is unique only to the true believers, then Christ's you-are-the-light-of-this-world teaching makes sense.

His peace quality, should we push it further, does not include any field of compromise in it. The true Christian is a peacemaker, but not a compromiser.

No Longer a Phenomenon: Born Again Makes One Understands the Gift of God

The greatest gift of God to the believers (aside from eternal life through faith in Jesus Christ) is the Holy Spirit. Christ said that God's Spirit will be with us forever. He is the Spirit of truth and "you know Him because He abides with and will be in you." (John 14:16-17) Then, another truth stated by John that the Holy Spirit flows like a river out of the true followers of Christ, the born-again Christians. (See John 7:37-39.)

When you speak to your friends as a Christian, your Holy Spirit will flow out of you like a river of positive wisdom and hope, but then their demons would get irritated because you speak the truth. Now we understand Christ's words: "Blessed are you when people insult you and persecute you, and falsely say all kinds of evil against you because of Me." (Matt. 5:11) It is the trait of the believer—a persecuted person in this demon-dominated world.

The Christian pretenders will never be ill-treated and harassed by their neighbors and friends since they share the same beliefs, philosophies, hopelessness, and hateful-to-God symptoms. The Spirit of truth does not know them.

Now, how to understand this Gift of God, which is the Holy Spirit? Well, we cannot understand God the Spirit, can we? We cannot fathom God, but we can experience the Holy Spirit.

For Christ said the Holy Spirit will teach us all things. The born-again Christian, for example, will not commit suicide because the Holy Spirit will equip him with divine wisdom and light during his darkest moments. (John 14:26)

The Holy Spirit will empower your biblical exhortation as when the people asked "Brethren, what shall we do?" after listening to Peter's sermon. Three thousand souls accepted and surrendered to Christ's lordship on this occasion because when they heard the message of truth, "they were pierced to the heart." (Acts 2:38)

Can we experience the Holy Spirit? Yes. When we felt uncomfortable with our sinful lives, it is the Holy Spirit convicting us of our sins. When we have a problem, but a solution presented itself after a season of prayer, then it is the Holy Spirit's intervention. (See Rom. 8:26-27)

The born-again Christian understands what God allows us to know about our relationship with His Spirit, who is living in our hearts.

9. CHRIST'S ALLUSION FROM THE OLD TESTAMENT'S BRONZE SERPENT

"And Moses made a bronze serpent and set it on the standard; and it came about, that if a serpent bit any man, when he looked to the bronze serpent, he lived." — Numbers 21:9.

The Bronze Serpent is Christ's Emblem for Sin

CHRIST TAUGHT NICODEMUS about Moses' bronze serpent in the wilderness, and He touched on the Israelites' sin of unbelief and how God forgave them by the former's believing or looking (by faith) at the bronze serpent hanging on a pole.

"As Moses lifted up the serpent in the wilderness," said Christ, "even so must the Son of Man be lifted up; so that whoever believes will in Him have eternal life. For God so loved the world, that He gave His only begotten Son, that whoever believes in Him shall not perish, but have eternal life." (John 3:14-16)

Note that around two-dozen verses held the conversation between Christ and Nicodemus in the book of John. They cover the popular verse John 3:16. All these statements spin around Christ's doctrine on how to enter heaven and live there forever.

To clear up Nicodemus' confusion, Christ used the Old Testament in Numbers 21 to point out how the born again doctrine tie in with man's complete and divine forgiveness.

One of God's well-known attributes is His utmost holiness. (See 1 Sam. 2:2, Hab. 1:13, etc.) Because of this, the "Lord sent fiery serpents among the people and they bit the people, so that many people of Israel died." (Num. 21:6) Nicodemus, during his conversation with Christ, may have sensed that the born again phenomenon could happen only if one would acknowledge his grave sinfulness before God's eyes.

The bronze serpent as discussed by Christ from the Book of Numbers could be His emblem for sin. Nicodemus, including all of us, should understand the second birth from God's hatred against sin so we can grasp the need for rebirth or regeneration to inherit eternal life.

The Bronze Serpent Unveils the Simplicity of Faith that Saves

Christ's allusion to the bronze serpent unveils the mystery of His cross and the doctrine of the second birth. While the carnal mind sees the second birth teaching with devilish contempt, the chosen ones in Christ are praising heaven for the utter simplicity of thought this doctrine brings.

During the Israelites' exodus from Egypt through Moses, there came a point where "the people spoke against God and Moses." They said, "Why have you brought us up out of Egypt to die in the wilderness? For there is no food and water, and we loathe this miserable food [manna]" (Num. 21:5). How did God quench their open rebellion? "And the Lord sent fiery serpents among the people and they bit the people, so that many people of Israel died" (Num. 21:6).

"So the people came to Moses and said, 'We have sinned, because we have spoken against the Lord and you; intercede with the Lord, that He may remove the serpents from us.... Then the Lord said to Moses, 'Make a fiery serpent, and set it on a standard; and it shall come about, that everyone who is bitten, when he looks at it, he shall live'" (Num. 21:7-8).

In a nutshell, we find that to be born again, based on Christ's analogy of the bronze serpent, is to look at Him, through the eyes of our heart; to look at the Lord bleeding on the cruel cross because of our sins.

Why did Christ use the bronze-serpent story when the Bible contains many God-punishing-sin stories? The answer is that it involves the hanging of the bronze serpent on a pole which is relevant to Christ's crucifixion. Here is Christ's statement to Nicodemus:

> "As Moses lifted up the serpent in the wilderness, even so must the Son of Man be lifted up; so that whoever believes will in Him have eternal life." (John 3:14-15)

Eternal life, according to Jesus, is achieved by trusting His finished work on the cross at Calvary as man's Redeemer for sin.

As the Israelites acknowledge their sin against God, so we too must acknowledge ours. Then let us look at Him—the Lord Jesus—in faith, who has the power to save us from the penalty of sin, which is eternal damnation in hell.

That is how to be born again if we believe Christ's words to Nicodemus over 2,000 years ago. It is merely looking at Him in faith as what the thief did at Calvary before he was saved and went with Christ in heaven. During Moses's time, those bitten by the fiery snakes were told to look at the bronze serpent on a pole to get healing and permanent cure.

The Bronze Serpent Typifies the Cruelty of Sin

To end God's death judgment because of the people's unbelief, the Israelites implored Moses to intercede. Then the LORD told him, "Make a replica of a poisonous snake and attach it to a pole. All who are bitten will live if they simply look at it!" (Num. 21:8, NLT) The born-again experience, therefore, involves Christ as our only Intercessor just as the Israelites had Moses to intercede for them. (See 1 Tim. 2:5) It is the biblical method to be born again: to look at Jesus by faith on the cruel cross since He bled and died for our sins. He sacrificed His own blood for our forgiveness!

This Bible teaching about the second birth is as easy to grasp as when Moses ordered the dying Jews to look at the bronze serpent to avoid death by a snake bite. We are sinners, like the Israelites, and we must acknowledge it as a terrible offense against our Maker. Second, God is Holy, and Christ came to intervene like Moses did so our Father would forgive us. If we would have this Scriptural faith of believing, as we would die should we persist in our unbelief, then it would cause our salvation and entrance to God's kingdom.

The bronze serpent typifies the cruelty of sin and God's judgment until one would look upon Jesus, who sacrificed and died for our transgressions. Looking upon that serpent on a pole to stop the flow of the deadly venom requires faith. It was pure faith!

In 2 Kings 18:4, however, God "broke in pieces the bronze serpent Moses had made" because the Israelites worshiped it. God is not a Catholic.

Well, can you imagine a man crawling and screaming in pain because of a killer snake bite? That is our case in the eyes of God regarding our sin. We cannot move; we cannot do good deeds anymore. Death in hell is just a breath away. It leaves us with nothing, except to look upon Jesus for help by faith. The thief on the cross did the same thing. (Cf. Luke 23:42-43)

The Bronze Serpent Mirrors the Cross of Jesus

As mentioned earlier, Christ expounded His born again doctrine from Numbers chapter 21. Many people died when God sent to them venomous snakes which bit the Israelites who murmured against the Exodus and the food, manna, which God provided. The power of sin wraps up our Lord's second birth teaching.

Do you want to enter the kingdom of God, Nicodemus? Well, let's talk first about your disqualification to live forever owing to your sinful nature. Therefore, you need to be born again.

Nicodemus said to Him, "How can a man be born when he is old? He cannot enter a second time into his mother's womb and be born, can he?" (John 3:4)

The shortcut to experience the second birth is genuine faith in Jesus as Savior and Redeemer. Like most people today, Nicodemus couldn't get it.

But why did Christ choose this historical record in Numbers, referring to Moses' bronze serpent to illustrate the second birth? Well, He told Nicodemus this incident, for it was the type of His own cross! Moses lifted the bronze serpent in the wilderness, just as Jesus got lifted and nailed on a cross. That whoever believes in our Lord may have eternal life.

It is worth repeating that trusting in Jesus is the key to heaven—the secret to being born again!

Remember that Christ opened His discussion with Nicodemus by saying: "Truly, truly, I say to you, unless one is born again, he cannot see the kingdom of God" (v. 3). There is only one requirement to be saved and to live forever in heaven: that is to be born again! Christ did not mention your self-righteousness and church activities.

To be born again as a requirement is like government employment for the native-born citizen only. No work if you are a foreigner. The same is true in heaven. No other passport being accepted there, except our born-again experience.

Perhaps Nicodemus left Christ that evening, understanding nothing. Christ's "Son of Man" sermon is always about Himself, but Nicodemus took it wrongly.

The Bronze Serpent Pictures the Role of Christ as Savior and Judge

The bronze serpent pictures the role of a savior and a judge. Why not a bronze dog or a bull? Well, it tells something about being judged (bitten) by the serpent and saved by the serpent. Man's Judge is Jesus Christ (Cf. Acts 17:31) who Himself is man's Savior. His judgment to the sinner is death, so He went to the cross to die for the sinner—to die a substitutionary death—to pay off the sinner's death penalty.

It explains Isaiah 53:5-6:

But He was pierced through for our transgressions, He was crushed for our iniquities; The chastening for our well-being fell upon Him, And by His scourging we are healed. All of us like sheep have gone astray, Each of us has turned to his own way; But the Lord has caused the iniquity of us all To fall on Him.

This is the Gospel, which has taught the born-again Christian to love Jesus, even if it would cause him his death. Christ is my Judge and Savior. He won't judge me if I would accept Him as my Savior. For this, Paul said, "Therefore there is now no condemnation for those who are in Christ Jesus." (Rom. 8:1)

Our Lord also said, "He who believes in Him is not judged; he who does not believe has been judged already, because he has not believed in the name of the only begotten Son of God." (John 3:18)

The born again doctrine is all about faith in Jesus. Our role is to believe, and we can do it!

10. THE KIND OF FAITH THAT LEADS TO THE SECOND BIRTH

Quite right, they were broken off for their unbelief, but you stand by your faith. Do not be conceited, but fear. — Romans 11:20.

WE HAVE DISCUSSED above the traits of the fake Christians such as hopelessness, prayerlessness, and the lack of a virtuous interest in the Word of God. Those who would become born-again Christians have also a recognizable pattern of faith or character.

The Faith that is Truth-Seeking

One cannot be born again who is a compromiser and an enemy of the truth. Christ urged us to "seek ye first the kingdom of God." Be a truth-seeker. Through His omniscience and foreknowledge, our Father God knew already if we would become His children by the second birth, even before the foundation of the world. To allow us all to repent and get saved, He sent Christ not just to die for our sins but also to enlighten us (See John 1:9) about our need for salvation. When there is a paper or preaching of His Word, for example, the Father would invite us to trust in Christ as Savior and Lord through convicting our consciences. "No one can come to Me unless the Father who sent Me draws him; and I will raise him up on the last day." (John 6:44)

This process would leave behind the "truth" rebels. God draws people for Himself, but not force them to believe. The hyper–Calvinists' insistence that we cannot exercise our free will is false teaching. (See Chapter 13 on Hyper-Calvinism) We need to seek and believe because God does not believe for us.

They argue that Christ resurrected Lazarus without asking the latter's agreement or free will. It is wrong since Lazarus was dead four days and dead people do not decide anymore.

I knew of a man who was a "seeker" of natural remedies away from home to cure his heart disease. He drained his resources by chasing after the quack doctors and their superstitions for decades. The interest in what is true or scientific never crossed his mind. I shared to him the Gospel, but his disinterest in the truth only thickened his unbelief. Long story short, he had a near-death experience, and from there became a seeker of Christ, urging his siblings to believe in Jesus before he died.

One poor farmer, for another illustration, met a heated discussion with a cult follower. He was humiliated and insulted as he could not defend the religion of his birth. Vowed to get back at the guy again, he sold a property and bought a Bible. Later, he became a pastor of a Christian church. He became a seeker of the truth after realizing his so-called religion was baseless—mere sinking sand!

After sharing to my mother the Gospel for a few minutes, and not meeting her again for months, she took the initiative in looking for a Christian church and there submitted to water baptism—without consulting me. Why had it happened so quickly? Because she was reading the Bible for years—she was a seeker of God.

There are countless testimonials about a truth-seeker meeting Christ at the end of the search. I experienced it; hence I knew it to work well in the second birth process.

The Faith that Responds to the Command to Believe

They said that salvation is a free gift and seeking the face of

God is unnecessary for the chosen ones. Yes, eternal life is free. It says in Romans 6:23 that "the free gift of God is eternal life in Jesus Christ our Lord." But the FAITH required in salvation is not free from God since "faith comes from hearing, and hearing by the word of Christ." (Rom. 10:17) We need to listen and hear and believe the Gospel. Remember the familiar Ephesians 2:8-9: "For by grace you have been saved through faith; and that not of yourselves, it is the gift of God; not as a result of works, so that no one may boast." God gave Jesus; hence salvation is a gift. But faith is not a gift, hence the command to believe. (See Acts 16:31) We need to be seekers of the truth with the free will to believe or not. If we are chosen to live in heaven by God's irresistible grace (as the hyper-Calvinists teach), then it could mean Christ does not love all. But such false teaching won't glorify Christ.

Predestination, as an extreme Calvinist's teaching, is blasphemous since it makes God the Author of sin and unjust. Is it not injustice to send billions of people to hell for the sin planned by God before the foundation of the world? Can you imagine being destined to hell because God hates you before the world began? Blasphemy.

God is love and salvation is given to us out of His love, but love dies without the freedom to love. Where is love after you kidnapped a girl and then marry her against her will? If salvation is rammed into our throat by predestination and God's overpowering grace, then heaven would cease to be a place of love, appreciation, worship, and praise, but it would rather become a home for the cold and thoughtless robotic people. No one would praise Jesus in heaven for what He did on the cross. That teaching is just unscriptural!

We learned from the Scriptures the need to respond in freedom to the command to believe and trust in Jesus, our Savior and Lord. (See John 3:16, 18, 36; Acts 16:31; Rom.

10:9-10)

The Faith that is Biblical

I have a relative who asked me how to get saved. After a brief exchange of chats and trivial arguments on Facebook, he turned sarcastic. His appetite for error could eat a horse. From such an experience, I realized the Word of God didn't reach his heart—he couldn't hear. So I gave up since a truth opposer is always insensible to things biblical.

King David pursued God's truths like no other. In the book of Psalms, he wrote: "Lead me in Your truth and teach me, For You are the God of my salvation; For You I wait all the day." (Ps. 25:5)

Do you want to be born again and know the mystery of the second birth? Be a truth seeker while you still have time to repent—not a controversial campaigner. When David asked God to "Lead me in your truth and teach me," he linked his truth-searching character with the "God of my salvation." The second birth is about your salvation from God's wrath, and to achieve it, Jesus wanted you to believe in a manner that you should:

"Ask, and it will be given to you; seek, and you will find; knock, and it will be opened to you. For everyone who asks receives, and the one who seeks finds, and to the one who knocks it will be opened." (Matt. 7:7-8)

Faith is not about arguing, but trust and humility before Christ. "Come to Me," our Lord invites us.

I had a friend who asked me about the exact verse of Christ's "I am the Way, and the Truth, and the Life." "John 14:6," I replied. Moments after, I heard him debating with his peers, making fun of the Bible as having many errors. Most people are "always learning and never able to come to the knowledge of the truth." (2 Tim. 3:7)

The second birth experience first happened with me when I took the Word of God like a hungry beggar gorging on bread. We don't have time for a debate when our sin-infected soul is desperate and craving for divine forgiveness by faith in Christ's atoning blood.

We are absorbed with God's Word that salvation is an urgent need. Such faith saves and assures one of life in heaven.

The Faith that Leads to Spiritual Transformation

I heard a Catholic relative insisting he is born again because he stopped smoking and drinking with friends. It was a typical argument for a lifestyle reformation just like dieting or the tired use of a new year's resolution, but the second birth phenomenon is a TRANSFORMATION (not just a mere reformation) that is made possible only through the intervention and indwelling of God's Spirit in your body. Concerning this divine transformation, the apostle Paul wrote: "Therefore if anyone is in Christ, he is a new creature; the old things passed away; behold, new things have come." (2 Cor. 5:17). It is deeper than the mere descriptive sketch of the best vocabulary in the English language. Think about the *old things* that have passed away, and the *new things* that have come. You will drain the Thesaurus in describing the second birth.

A believer is transformed by the Spirit of God.

The Faith that is Experiential

After His resurrection, Christ "breathed on them and said to them, 'Receive the Holy Spirit.'" (John 20:22) Christ is God, otherwise, He could not have breathed God the Spirit into His disciples. This episode corresponds to Christ's teaching in John 3 that one needs to be born again to enter God's kingdom. When Jesus taught Nicodemus the doctrine of the second birth as the only requisite to enter heaven, he said, "The wind blows where it wishes, and you hear its sound, but you do not know where it comes from or where it goes. So it is with everyone who is born of the Spirit." (John 3:8) The second birth is an encounter like the wind blows. I can write it since I experienced it.

The preacher (I listened to during a church service) talked about sin, God's wrath and the judgment to come because of it, and God's grace by sending His Son, Jesus, to save us from sin through His shed blood on the cross. My heart got so touched by Jesus for the first time. He died for me—I felt a love for Him in a flash! I appreciated His sacrifices for me; I wanted to follow Him. Then the pastor asked us to open our hearts for Jesus and receive Him as our only Lord and Savior from sin. And I did it; I prayed for Jesus to come into my heart and assuage my unhappy and confused life.

After that experience one Sunday morning I became a new man, and "So it is with everyone who is born of the Spirit." The Spirit of Christ has lived in my soul since 1984, and He has never left me since then. It is a sweet relationship with the Son of God in my soul, while my unbelieving relatives and friends mocked me as I distanced myself already from our drinking and joking sessions and nonsense discussions. The Spirit of God in my soul transformed me and I knew it—hence, my writing about it!

The mystery of the second birth ceases to be so after meeting Jesus by faith and personally living the born-again experience. It is no longer mysterious for me. I knew it. Romans 8:9 is one of my favorite Bible verses. Wrote the apostle Paul: "However, you are not in the flesh but in the

Spirit, if indeed the Spirit of God dwells in you. But if anyone does not have the Spirit of Christ, he does not belong to Him." In this verse alone, Paul talked about God the Spirit, God the Father, and God the Son. What's the point, Paul? Well, your body and soul become the home of the triune God once you accept Jesus into your heart by faith that He died as a ransom to take your sins away forever! That's who you are if you are born again. You are the temple of God—a new person indeed!

Sad that the fake Christian does not know it.

The Faith that Trusts the Bible as the Writings of the Living God

True Christians love and defend the Holy Scriptures. It is the breath and heartbeat of their relationship with Christ. Remove the Bible or twist it if you want to raise false Christians in your church. Testified a pseudo-Christian lawyer, for example, that his heart palpitated as he talked with the Philippine "I-am-the-Christ" cult leader (his name is not worth promoting). It is the sad song of an educated guy ignorant of the Scriptures. But the cults cannot deceive the born-again Christians because of their devotion to the *Sacred Writings* of the prophets and apostles of God. No iota of Darwinism in the back of their mind.

To the born-again believers in Thessalonica, the apostle Paul wrote that he constantly thanked God because when he preached the word of God, "you accepted it not as the word of men, but for what it really is, the WORD OF GOD, which also performs its work in you who believe." (1 Thess. 2:13) The Scripture is the Word of God and it works on the believers.

"Your word is a lamp to my feet," wrote the psalmist, "And a light to my path." (Psalm 119:105) The born-again Christians believe the Bible like it is God talking to them when they read it. This quality of faith also finds a trace in Psalm 119:38:

"Establish Your word to Your servant, As that which produces reverence for You."

You venerate God because you trusted in the Holy Bible's authority. The Liberal Christians are just busy discrediting the Scriptures for their lack of understanding. Christ said no truth will dawn on those having no Spirit of God in their souls.

Like a dead leaf dancing with the wave—that is the Christian pretender! The Word of God does not bear any seal of authority for him. If he hears the church say "Amen," he would join the chorus without rhyme or reason.

The Bible scholar, who is a fake Christian, studies God's Word to slander it. It is how the liberals attack the Bible in the guise of intellectual expertise. One pastor who has mastered the Greek language preached on a Wednesday Prayer Meeting that God does not need our worship. When pressed on John 4:23 which teaches that the Father even seeks for people to worship Him, the pastor retorted: "The Bible has so many errors!" That's how a flimflammer unmasks his Christian pretensions. But the born-again follower of Jesus will always have a delight in his heart for the Word of God. Wrote the psalmist: "Your statutes are my songs In the house of my pilgrimage." (Psalm 119:54)

Concerning the Holy Bible, C. H. Spurgeon said, "This volume is the writing of the living God; each letter was penned with an Almighty finger; each word in it dropped from the everlasting lips; each sentence was dictated by the Holy Spirit." It is the faith of the genuine Christian that the fake one does not have.

The Bible is the writing of the living God!

The Faith that Produces a Living Relationship with Jesus

We have seen some Facebook posts arguing eternal life's assurance through a relationship with Christ. From the Web, we found this definition: "Religion is belief in a god or gods and the activities that are connected with this belief, such as praying or worshipping in a building such as a church or temple." In short, all may have a religion (a belief in a god), but not all have a living relationship with Christ.

The demons, for example, believe in God and shudder (Cf. James 2:19) but they don't believe in the claims of Christ.

Since Christ is the Way to the Father, we make no option but Christ alone to gain eternal life and entrance to heaven.

Our Lord taught Nicodemus this truth: "[E]ven so must the Son of Man be lifted up; so that whoever believes will in Him have eternal life." (John 3:14b-15) A relationship with Christ starts with believing Him (not just believing "about" Him) and trusting His promises.

The outcome of believing was best described by the apostle Paul in Galatians 2:20. He wrote: "I have been crucified with Christ; and it is no longer I who live, but CHRIST LIVES IN ME; and the life which I now live in the flesh I live by faith in the Son of God, who loved me and gave Himself up for me." In only four words, Paul penned the doctrine on our attachment to Christ: "Christ lives in me." The fake Christian cannot testify to this brand of closeness with Christ.

Note that Paul's "faith in the Son of God" got its root after experiencing Christ's love. What is this love? Well, he said, Christ "gave Himself up for me." Or Christ died for me on the cross! It is the Gospel. For an exhaustive understanding of what Jesus did for us, observe Isaiah's prophecy around 700 years before Christ's birth:

> *But He was pierced through for our transgressions,*
> *He was crushed for our iniquities;*
> *The chastening for our well-being fell upon Him,*
> *And by His scourging we are healed. (Is. 53:5)*

Who won't love Christ for what He did to our souls, to ransom our sins by His own blood? The nominal Christians. Yes, they will never love Jesus, for they are no different from the pure unbelievers. They don't have a living relationship with Christ since they are unrepentant sinners and rejecters of Jesus. Christ is not Lord for them!

The Faith that Yields to Christ's Lordship

Have you noticed a church pastor who is a pseudo-Christian? There are thousands of them among the liberals. Observe this headline from Christianity Today (October 9, 2015): "The world's first lesbian bishop of a major Christian denomination, Eva Brunne of the Lutheran Church of Sweden is calling for the removal of the crosses and other Christian symbols at the Seamen's Church in Freeport so that visiting foreign sailors practicing other religions like Islam 'would not be offended.'"[25]

First, the liberal Christians ordained a woman as their bishop, which is unscriptural (1 Tim. 2:12). Second, they don't want to offend people when the Gospel always offends the unbelievers. (1 Cor. 1:18, 23) When the doctrine is man-made,

---

[25] Ong, Czarina. Lesbian bishop wants to remove church crosses so Muslims 'won't be offended.' Christianitytoday.com.https://www.christiantoday.com/article/lesbian-bishop-wants-to-remove-church-crosses-so-muslims-wont-be-offended/66831.htm (accessed May 3, 2020).

political correctness rules among the fake Christians. A living relationship with Christ will never happen when church leaders vilify the Word of God and refuse Christ's lordship.

For the born-again Christian, our relationship with Christ is real oneness as our attachment with our family except for the human element in the familial context like misunderstanding, greed, self-interest, etc.

Aside from Christ's Spirit's indwelling (Cf. Rom. 8:9), our Lord said in John 15:5: "I am the vine, you are the branches; he who abides in Me and I in him, he bears much fruit, for apart from Me you can do nothing." Our relationship with our Savior Jesus is akin to the vine and its branches that border on true dependence just as the branches hinge themselves on the trunk. The Christian pretender does not experience such closeness with our Lord.

I met a false Christian one day. He smiled and chuckled as I shared with him some Bible verses and how they heightened my experience with our Lord. He couldn't tie in with my Christian witness. His unbelief unmasked itself just like the familiar caught-on-the-act unfolding of the incurable liars. The chorus of the born-again Christians in praising their Lord never entered his heart!

The Faith that Breeds Answered Prayers

The born-again Christian will always tell you he had his prayers answered by Christ. In John 15:5 our Lord said that without Him we can do nothing. Hence, He obliged Himself to answer His children. Two verses after it, He taught that "If you abide in Me, and My words abide in you, ask whatever you wish, and it will be done for you." (John 15:7)

Christ also directed us to, "Ask, and it will be given to you; seek, and you will find; knock, and it will be opened to you." (Matt. 7:7) A prominent part of Christ's nature is to answer our prayers after we abide in Him and His words.

The false believers would never live with Christ and in His promises. Their prayers are meaningless to them as they don't even expect Christ to hear them. They are just faithless—pretending to be one with Christ's followers. When you pray outside of faith, your prayers become words of sarcasm and hypocrisy just like sending things to heaven abominable to God. Wrote John that "God does not hear sinners." (John 9:31a)

Here is how the prophet Isaiah taught about God's rejection of the prayers of the pseudo-believers:

> But your iniquities have made a separation between you and your God, And your sins have hidden His face from you so that He does not hear. (Is. 59:2)

The Faith that Trusts Christ Completely

A person who is not born of God is unsaved and unforgiven. The nominal Christians are one of them. Their sins have separated them from God and have caused God to ignore their prayers. Of the real Christians, the apostle Paul said, "In Him [Christ] we have redemption through His blood, the forgiveness of our trespasses, according to the riches of His grace." (Eph. 1:7)

Our faith in Christ's atoning blood—as born-again Christians—reconciles us to God. (See 2 Cor. 5:18) We are no longer separated from God. Our prayers can now reach heaven because of Jesus, our Forgiver, and Mediator.

I am so absorbed by this teaching that my life became a give-me-this-Lord existence. I remember one author who stressed that Christ, during His humanity, received everything from His Father through the medium of prayer. The camouflage Christians do not know the power of prayer, and the saddest part of their situation is they expect to enter heaven one day. Of these fakers Christ said, "Many will say to Me on that day, 'Lord, Lord . . .' And then I will declare to them, 'I never knew you; depart from Me.'" (Matt. 7:21-22)

Unless you are a praying Christian, you can never share your story. Unreconciled with God, unbelief knows no answered prayer.

My wife was about to pass the age of childbearing when we realized we had only two sons but no daughter. For nine months we prayed every morning (even day and night sometimes) that our Lord Jesus would give us a daughter. In those days, ultrasound technology was still unknown in tiny towns such as ours. The day to give birth arrived, and Christ gave us a beautiful baby girl.

The answered prayers of the true Christian are an endless narrative among the believers. Those members of the fake Christian movement have no answered prayer to tell since Christ never knew them.

11. THE ASSURANCE OF THE BORN-AGAIN BELIEVER

"[A]nd I give eternal life to them, and they will never perish; and no one will snatch them out of My hand." — John 10:28.

THE BORN-AGAIN CHRISTIAN is assured of eternal salvation if we were to invite Christ to speak to us, for He said, "I give eternal life to them, and they will never perish." (John 10:28) I had a friend who told me his seminary rejected eternal security, but he found the truth from the Scriptures anyway in the course of his study as a preacher.

Assured Because Salvation is a Gift from God

A born-again Christian who rejects this precious doctrine of "once saved, always saved" is one who's anemic in doctrine; most of them are not serious Bible students. If you knew God and believed in His Word, you would never doubt that He "gave Himself for us to redeem us from every lawless deed, and to purify for Himself a people for His own possession." (Tit. 2:14) God wills to have a redeemed people for His own name—He's purifying them! It is the bedrock of our immortality in heaven. It is God's blueprint for the eternal realm: To seal up His own chosen ones by faith in Christ! (Cf. 2 Cor. 1:22; Eph. 1:13)

Most people believed they could please God by their self-righteousness and perfect church attendance. But the prophet Isaiah said: "We are all infected and impure with sin. When we display our righteous deeds, they are nothing but filthy rags." (Is. 64:6, NLT) Our assurance of immortality is not based on our ability to appear sinless before God for perfection is impossible in this life.

A friend told me he had been giving enormous sums to his church. From God's standpoint, however, we are sinners, and our good deeds can never solve our spiritual deadlock with our Maker. So, God came down through Christ to make our forgiveness possible. Wrote John: "In this is love, not that we loved God, but that He loved us and sent His Son to be the propitiation [or perfect blood offering] for our sins." (1 John 4:10) God is holy, and we are sinners. We need a mediator and a savior of our transgressions, who is Christ, our Lord. (Cf. 1 Tim. 2:5)

Give all your wealth to the charitable institutions, for example, then return home poor and still guilty of breaking God's foremost law, which is to love Him with all your mind, heart, soul, and strength. (See Mark 12:30) We're not perfect. You can give without loving. You can give out everything to satisfy your self-esteem, but you cannot love God outside of Christ.

The rich young Ruler, for example, asked—after declaring he obeyed all the commandments—how to inherit eternal life. Christ said, sell your wealth and follow me. The Ruler refused. He obeyed God's command, he claimed, but couldn't love and follow Jesus. It is the point. The only method to get God's salvation is God's method, which is stonewalled with our assurance of eternal life. What is this method? John 3:16 provides the answer, that whoever believes in Jesus "shall not perish, but have eternal life." Wrote the apostle Paul:

> For I am convinced that neither death, nor life, nor angels, nor principalities, nor things present, nor things to come, nor powers, nor height, nor depth, nor any other created thing, will be able to separate us from the love of God, which is in Christ Jesus our Lord." (Rom. 8:38-39)

Note that we will have the assurance of salvation—God's love won't separate us from Him; and IN CHRIST JESUS OUR LORD alone!

Assured Because the Redeemed People are God's

Angel Gabriel told Mary that Jesus would reign in His kingdom on earth forever. (Luke 1:31b-33) And in other related Scriptures, we, the born-again Christians (together with the O.T. and the Tribulation saints), will reign with Him as "kings and priests." Note these verses in the Book of Revelation:

> And hath made us kings and priests unto God and his Father; to him be glory and dominion for ever and ever. And hast made us unto our God kings and priests: and we shall reign on the earth . . .and they shall reign for ever and ever." (Rev. 1:6; 5:10; 22:5b, KJV)

The point is clear. God has laid His plans in eternity future, and He cannot just leave the followers of Christ to their own defenses from the "flaming missiles" of the evil one. He will hold my hand up to ensure the fulfillment of His plans for me, the believer. The apostle Peter wrote that we are a chosen race, a royal priesthood, a holy nation, a people for God's own possession. (1 Pet. 2:9-10)

Now we understand why Christ taught that the good slave would "be in authority over ten cities.'" (Cf. Luke 19:17) We will become the administrators of Christ's kingdom on earth as bondservants of the Lord. Our preservation as the people of God fills the Holy Scriptures.

Assured Because We Cannot Maintain What We don't Produce

From the start of this paper, we underscored the biblical truth that God's grace offers us free eternal salvation. Wrote Paul that God's grace (or undeserved kindness) saves us through our faith in Jesus and not according to our good works, so we won't boast. (Cf. Eph. 2:8-9) Salvation is God's gift through trusting in Christ as Savior and Lord since "the free gift of God is eternal life" in Jesus. (Rom. 6:23b) Rejection of Christ, therefore, is equivalent to accepting God's hell judgment. Christ Himself taught it: "he who does not believe has been judged already, because he has not believed in the name of the only begotten Son of God." (John 3:18b)

Why is salvation a gift? The reason is the holiness of God and the Law's perfect nature versus man's inherent imperfection. God's holiness calls for man's savior, hence the incarnation of God the Son, Jesus. The apostle Paul wrote to the Galatians that obedience to the Law cannot make a man righteous; only faith in Christ can. (Cf. Gal. 2:16)

Early on, from the Old Testament story in Genesis 15, the Bible said that God credited Abraham's faith as evidence of righteousness. In Romans 4, Paul said that if works of righteousness had justified Abraham, he would have something to boast about. I heard people boasting about their generosity to the church. We don't have a problem with that, except that our soul's salvation cannot happen by giving away cash. We cannot buy eternal life. Heaven does not need our money.

Hebrews chapter 11 (the faith Chapter) records how the faith of the saints shaped the records of the entire Scriptures. Our saints from the OT down to the New Testament got martyred for their faith. God honored our faith more than our deeds of righteousness for the Lord's service. Paul even went to say, "as it is written, 'THERE IS NONE RIGHTEOUS, NOT EVEN ONE.'"

Our self-righteousness is just inadequate to secure immortality.

Understanding the eternal salvation of our souls, we can now substantiate further our premise that our assurance of heaven is a logical, let alone biblical, possibility as it came from God Himself for free by faith in Christ.

Paul said: "I do not nullify the grace of God, for if righteousness comes through the Law, then Christ died needlessly." (Gal. 2:21) It is the doctrine. If we can maintain our salvation by our human efforts to cling unto God, then Christ's atoning sacrifice at Calvary is just a waste of precious blood.

The biblical teaching is that our salvation is free from God by faith in Christ's substitutionary death to pay off our sins. That said, the burden to maintain our salvation is now on God's side. Our Father in heaven assures us of eternal life based on the truth that our immortality originates from His grace.

From this scriptural ground, we can now see Christ's teaching in John 10 under a new lens of clarity:

"I give eternal life to them, and they will never perish; and no one will snatch them out of My hand. My Father, who has given them to Me, is greater than all; and no one is able to snatch them out of the Father's hand. I and the Father are one." (John 10:28-30)

Salvation is God's free gift (grace), which we receive through our genuine faith in Christ and His promises, as already mentioned. "For by grace you have been saved through faith." Once the salvation process got completed by believing in Jesus, our Lord would justify and save us from the penalty of sin, which is death in hell. "Therefore," taught Paul, "there is now no condemnation for those who are in Christ Jesus." (Rom. 8:1)

But what if we sinned against God? Well, note that after our salvation, which we also termed in this paper as the born again event, the next phase in our Christian experience is sanctification or Christian living. As born-again followers of Jesus, we will have dominion and power over sin. "For sin shall not be master over you, for you are not under law but under grace." (Rom. 6:14)

The three stages of the born-again experience are SALVATION (salvation from the penalty of sin); SANCTIFICATION (salvation from the power of sin); and GLORIFICATION (salvation from the presence of sin). Let's go back to our question. What if we sinned? Well, sinning after salvation falls under SANCTIFICATION (set apart) or Christian living. The apostle Peter, for example, followed Jesus (received salvation) and then denied our Lord (failed in sanctification)—or he failed to walk by faith! Had he died after his "rooster crows" denials, Peter would still wake up in heaven like the Thief on the cross who hadn't had the luxury of time to live the born-again life.

We maintain our position that sinful Peter did not lose his salvation after denying Jesus since he confessed his sins, "And he went out and wept bitterly." (Luke 22:62) Our authentic conversion to the Christian faith, despite our imperfections, guarantees our eternal life since Christ said, "no one will snatch them out of My hand."

I have friends who cannot digest this biblical teaching. We cannot maintain our divine salvation since we don't produce it. In salvation, we are justified or declared righteous already by God. "For we maintain," taught Paul, "that a man is justified by faith apart from works of the Law." (Rom. 3:28)

In sanctification, we sometimes sin. (1 John 1:8) If we don't sin, the truth is not in us. (1 John 1:9) But "If we confess our sins, He is faithful and righteous to forgive us our sins and to cleanse us from all unrighteousness."

What's the point? In sanctification, we walk by faith not by sight (2 Cor. 5:7). How? By the intervention of our Lord Jesus Christ and His Spirit. Observe what I call the COVID-19 verses (the popular Scripture during the China virus!):

> "In the same way the Spirit also helps our weakness; for we do not know how to pray as we should, but the Spirit Himself intercedes for us with groanings too deep for words; and He who searches the hearts knows what the mind of the Spirit is, because He intercedes for the saints according to the will of God. And we know that God causes all things to work together for good to those who love God, to those who are called according to His purpose." (Rom. 8:26-28)

We have victory over sin as we live the born-again life since "God is faithful, and he will not let you be tempted beyond your ability." (1 Cor. 10:13, ESV)

Regarding our assurance of salvation, we have the guarantee of waking up in heaven. Concerning sanctification, we also have a divine promise of victory over sin.

The born-again Christian experiences security in the arms of Jesus, our Lord. A troubled and shaky Christian spiritually is not a born-again "believer" of Christ at all, as no one would mistrust Jesus after tasting God's Spirit in our soul. Note Hebrews 6:

> "For in the case of those who have once been enlightened and have tasted of the heavenly gift and have been made partakers of the Holy Spirit, and have tasted the good word of God and

the powers of the age to come, and then have fallen away, it is impossible to renew them again to repentance, since they again crucify to themselves the Son of God and put Him to open shame." (Heb. 6:4-6)

So clear that God assures the genuine born-again Christian of salvation and victory over sin since he is never an on and off believer.

What about the backslider? Well, all things would be turbulent for him as with the prodigal son, but he would repent and return. Since John said, "They went out from us, but they were not really of us; for if they had been of us, they would have remained with us; but they went out, so that it would be shown that they all are not of us." (1 John 2:19)

The habitual backslider is a Christian apostate. He is not a born-again believer.

We covered the fake Christian somewhere in this book.

Assured Because It is a Scriptural Promise

I searched through Google commentaries supporting the Arminian doctrine of earning salvation by self-righteousness but found almost nothing from the search results on page one of the browsers. Without a scriptural doctrine on how we are saved from hell, we could never see the corresponding eternal security enclosed in the biblical salvation teaching. In John 17, for example, Christ said His followers "are not of the world, even as I am not of the world." He didn't say, "Father, we are unsure if they could maintain their saved condition."

John Wesley honored all Scriptures involving salvation by grace but insisted on perfect sanctification as possible in our lifetime. He preached it but admitted he had not attained it. Hence, the safe path to follow is biblical salvation by faith alone, and with it our guarantee from falling away through the intervention of God. The Bible teaches that we won't fall away as it is equivalent to crucifying Christ again and putting Him to open shame.

If we go on sinning willfully, states the Epistle to the Hebrews, expect God's terrifying judgment (v. 26). But in the last part of Hebrews 10, it says, "we are not of those who shrink back to destruction." (Heb. 10:26, 39)

The Bible is a Supernatural Book. If we would say that by His grace God gave us salvation through faith, our Lord also said, "Therefore you are to be perfect, as your heavenly Father is perfect." (Matt. 5:48) Again, this verse falls under Christian Living or Sanctification, not Salvation, since Christ is the Way to Heaven, not our perfection and self-righteousness. Second, the most used verse by the Arminians (the proponents of the good-works Theology) is in Matthew 24:13. It says, "But the one who endures to the end, he will be saved."

These issues baffle the young believers. First, concerning Christian practice in Matthew 5:48, we strive to live holy lives. But, as mentioned already, it is sanctification, and not justification (or divine forgiveness or salvation). Another point. Matthew 24:13 refers to the endurance during the Great Tribulation, which is another story. It is not about the salvation of our souls.

The promised assurance of salvation floods the Holy Scriptures. (See John 10:27-30; 3:3; 3:16; 1 John 5:13; Rom. 5:1; 8:31-39; Eph. 1:13-14; Heb. 6:18-20; 7:25—we cannot list them all!) Hebrews 7:25 punctuates on the reasons of our assurance, which are Christ's authority and intercession. "Therefore," reads the verse, "He is able also to save forever those who draw near to God through Him, since He always lives to make intercession for them."

Now, First Corinthians 10:13 turns easy to comprehend:

"No temptation has overtaken you but such as is common to man; and God is faithful, who will not allow you to be tempted beyond what you are able, but with the temptation will provide the way of escape also, so that you will be able to endure it."

A heated debate among preachers about eternal security occurred during a Bible study session, for which one pastor said, "Why not invite Christ into the discussion?" Then he read John 10:28:

"[A]nd I give eternal life to them, and they will never perish; and no one will snatch them out of My hand."

This verse silenced them all.

The Bible teaches the preservation of our salvation and eternal life. Christ Himself taught it—we cannot dispute it!

12. OUR DIVINE SONSHIP AS BORN-AGAIN CHRISTIANS

For you are all sons of God through faith in Christ Jesus. — Galatians 3:26.

FAITH IN CHRIST is the most wonderful and powerful phrase ever invented in the English language. It is a worn-out locution for the unbelievers as they are used to saying "faith in Bruce Lee" or "faith in Trump" with no spiritual value in it. Anything attached to Jesus Christ, however, beams with a sacred overtone. In John 10:28, for an example, Christ said: "I give eternal life to them, and they will never perish; and no one will snatch them out of My hand."

Belief in Christ stands for eternal life after death; and in this life, a promise that you will never perish and that no one can separate you from His love and protection.

Thus, faith in Christ is a loaded thing. God even called Christ's followers His children and heirs with Jesus Christ. This is how the apostle Paul puts it:

"The Spirit Himself testifies with our spirit that we are children of God, and if children, heirs also, heirs of God and fellow heirs with Christ, if indeed we suffer with Him so that we may also be glorified with Him." (Rom. 8:16-17)

We are sons of the living God if we believe our Lord Jesus. The pleasant news is that such a divine relationship knows no expiration. No sickness or any circumstance—even in the hour of death—can severe it. Our adoption as children of God lasts forever since "whoever believes in Him [Christ] shall not perish, but have eternal life." (John 3:16)

The apostle Paul also said: "For you are all sons of God

through faith in Christ Jesus." (Gal. 3:26)

Our Divine Sonship Guarantees Christ's Lordship

Elsewhere in this work, I wrote that heaven requires the second birth, and we experience it after accepting Jesus as Lord into our hearts.

In my acquaintances, I noticed the doctrine of receiving Christ as Lord into one's life getting obscure and ill-defined. Many don't realize that the acceptance of Christ's Spirit is also the affirmation of His lordship and rule over our body and soul. Here is one specimen of this confusion. In First Corinthians 10:13, Paul said: "No temptation has overtaken you but such as is common to man; and God is faithful, who will not allow you to be tempted beyond what you are able, but with the temptation will provide the way of escape also, so that you will be able to endure it." God does not try the born-again Christian with sufferings or temptations he can't subdue. Someone asked me: "How can we escape before a beautiful woman?" "God will fight for you," I replied. That's the gist of the Word of God in First Corinthians 10:13.

Most Christians misunderstand Christ's lordship. The Bible said God will not allow you to be tempted. It is God who will rescue you. You won't resist your temptation by your own human efforts or philosophies. God will be there to defend you, as He did with Joseph from Potiphar's wife's sexual assaults. (See Gen. 39.)

Your trials will crush you to pieces only when Christ is not Lord in your life—only when Christ is not King in your heart!

A born-again Christian is victorious because he is a child of God. John said: "For whatever is born of God overcomes the world; and this is the victory that has overcome the world—our faith."

Divine sonship begins with salvation, which is Christ's Spirit's indwelling in your soul. Lordship salvation is the phrase used to describe Christ's rule in the believer's life in contrast to easy-believism. God's child is like a sheep obeying the Shepherd, Jesus, who will rule him with the rod of discipline in the vineyard of His grace and love.

Our Divine Sonship Guarantees Our Humility and Repentant Attitude toward God

Repentance is the other side of faith. Without it, your faith cannot stand. It is akin to a hypertensive person who is eating foods high in unhealthy fat after believing he had high blood pressure. It is easy-believism when your doctor tells you to stop smoking, but you continue to smoke after the warning. You believe, no problem, but you won't obey. When you sinned, you wouldn't repent; you would not have a "godly sorrow"!

In Christianity, this meaningless faith is just a mere spiritual assent, not a rebirth because a genuine born-again experience happens only after submission to Christ's authority. You cannot accept Christ as your Lord in your lips, but not in your heart. Hence, in 2nd Corinthians 5:17, Paul said, "Therefore if anyone is in Christ, he is a new creature; the old things passed away; behold, new things have come."

Without newness in your soul, you are not a born-again Christian. The children of God are "new creatures." A repentant confession to God dries out their sins with Christ's forgiveness. It is our divine sonship that glues our sweet relationship with God in Christ.

Our Divine Sonship Guarantees Our Godly Lives

I am against sinless perfection because we are all sinners even after our born-again experience. John said, "If we say we have no sin, we deceive ourselves, and the truth is not in us . . .. If we say we have not sinned, we make him a liar, and his word is not in us." (1 John 1:8, 10) These words load with anti-perfectionism.

God said we sin occasionally, but we are not "slaves to sin." (Rom. 6:6) "For sin shall not be master over you, for you are not under law but under grace." (Rom. 6:14)

We cannot live the life of sin (like having two wives, for example) as children of God, because His grace won't allow it. He would not allow the temptation to catch us beyond our ability to endure. (1 Cor. 10:13) God intervenes through the agency of His grace to help us live the godly life.

Positionally, God sanctifies us (or sets us apart) because of Christ. We find it in Hebrews 10:10: "By this will we have been sanctified through the offering of the body of Jesus Christ once for all." (See also 2 Thess. 2:13; 1 Cor. 6:11.)

Second, we "shall all be taught of God." (John 6:45) The Holy Spirit in our body will teach us all things. (John 14:26) Hence, we can live a life without conforming to this world. (Rom. 12:2) Theologians call it practical or progressive sanctification.

The bottom line is that to live a godly life is possible as children of God. Our divine sonship guarantees our godly existence.

In Romans 8, Paul said that we walk according to Christ's Spirit if we are children of God. (v.9)

The pseudo-Christians cannot live the life controlled by God's Spirit because they set their minds on the flesh. They give God displeasure because of their hostility toward

Him. (Rom. 8:6-8)

Our Divine Sonship Guarantees Our Heavenly Blessings

The apostle Paul wrote in Ephesians about the blessings of the born-again Christians. He said we have "every spiritual blessing in the heavenly places in Christ." (Eph. 1:3) From this topic sentence, he enumerated these blessings from our sonship down to all other sacred favors. He discussed our redemption, heavenly inheritance, and the sealing off of the Holy Spirit as the signature of our birthright as children of God.

After hearing the Ephesians' faith in Christ, Paul said, he did not cease to mention in his prayers that God will give them more wisdom and knowledge about Christ. (Eph. 1:15-18) Paul knew the bearings of the followers of Christ. He thanked God for their faith. "For this reason I too," wrote Paul, "having heard of the faith in the Lord Jesus which exists among you . . . do not cease giving thanks for you, while making mention of you in my prayers." (Eph. 1:15-16)

The immense blessing of divine sonship is not just the eternal assurance of redemption, but a flood of guarantees while still living in this life. Wrote John: "Beloved, I pray that in all respects you may prosper and be in good health, just as your soul prospers." (3 John 1:2) Christ also said, "Blessed are they who did not see, and yet believed." (John 20:29b)

But what captivated my soul more is Christ's intercession. When I'm hungry, our Lord is there for me to quench my need; when I'm full, He's still there for me to lift my spirit and thank the Lord.

My wife and I prayed persistently for Christ's intervention during the COVID-19. We asked our Lord Jesus to help us restart our livelihood from scratch. And He intervened. Then after 2020, we got exposed to COVID-19, which killed one of our closest relatives. His grace and mercy to our extensive family saved us from the infection. Praise the Name of our Lord Jesus!

Our Divine Sonship Guarantees Growth and Spiritual Discernment

A born-again Christian is a fruit-bearing follower of Christ. "And the one on whom seed was sown on the good soil," taught our Lord, "this is the man who hears the word and understands it; who indeed bears fruit and brings forth, some a hundredfold, some sixty, and some thirty." (Matt. 13:23)

In Christ's Parable of the Sower, He taught some have God's Word taken away from their hearts by the devil, and others have faith that does not have roots. Only those who understood the Gospel could bear much fruit. And in Mark 11:21, Christ cursed the fruitless fig tree, and it died. Growth in faith always follows genuine Christianity.

It is impossible to claim salvation without a regenerated soul. To validate this spiritual rebirth, God gifted the one having a genuine conversion to the Christian faith with spiritual discernment. With divine sonship, the Holy Spirit can now teach the reborn Christian "all things." Nicodemus appeared confused during his conversation with Jesus. Later, he joined Joseph of Arimathea in preparing for Christ's burial. He got converted and developed a sound spiritual judgment.

I had a church friend who left his job since his coworkers were unbelievers. After a while, his son quit school, his family starving. This guy didn't have spiritual discernment, for Christ said, "I do not ask You to take them out of the world, but to keep them from the evil one." (John 17:15) No problem working with the non-Christians according to our Lord.

When God says, "'Come out and be separate,'" wrote John Charles Ryle, "this does not mean that Christians should give up their work in the world. Cornelius the soldier, Luke the doctor and Zenas the lawyer are examples of men in secular work. In fact, it is sinful to be idle, and idleness often leads us into temptation. So it is right that we should have a lawful job of work. We must not give up any occupation (unless it is sinful in and of itself) out of fear that it will harm us. That is lazy and cowardly conduct. What we ought to do is to take our Christianity with us into our places of employment in the world."[26]

Divine sonship is just equivalent to a godly judgment. Some born-again Christians, however, are babes in Christ. They don't have Spirit-guided lives. I met people who were Christians for decades but know nothing about the Scriptures. These guys do not represent born-again Christianity. For Christ said, "So every good tree bears good fruit, but the bad tree bears bad fruit." (Matt. 7:17) This metaphor follows growth since fruit-bearing trees are grownup trees. Second, growth requires food (or fertilizer, as with the trees), which is the Word of God since we shall live "ON EVERY WORD THAT PROCEEDS OUT OF THE MOUTH OF GOD." (Matt. 4:4)

We expect a change in the life of a born-again child of God. (2 Cor. 5:17) Easy-believism is not biblical from the context of repentance. After rebirth is submission to Christ's lordship. Wrote Paul, "and He died for all, so that they who live might no longer live for themselves, but for Him who died and rose again on their behalf." (2 Cor. 5:15)

---

26 Ryle, J. C. "Walking with God." Classicbiblestudyguide.com. http://classicbiblestudyguide.com/English/WalkingWithGod.pdf, p.30.

Spiritual discernment proves divine sonship. A Christian person voting for a questionable character, for example, lacks a godly judgment. A fogged discernment demeans divine sonship.

13. OF THE HYPER-CALVINIST'S HERESY

*When the Gentiles heard this, they began
rejoicing and glorifying the word of the Lord;
and as many as had been appointed to eternal life
believed. — Acts 13:48.*

I WANT TO manifest I am not against Calvinism if we mean "salvation by faith," and not by good deeds and self-righteousness. But I am opposed to 5-Point Calvinism, which is a combination of five teachings that cannot stand without the support of the other related points. This doctrine kills off soul winning and adorns predestination. It also invents a man-made doctrine known as BORN AGAIN TO BELIEVE. This persuasion is termed as Hyper-Calvinism.

I find this Chapter close to my heart because I have close friends from this persuasion who taught that faith happens after the born-again experience—or **born again to believe**! Martyn Lloyd-Jones once said, "We do not give birth to ourselves, we are not reborn because we believe. We believe because we are reborn."[27]

First off, what if we would invite Nicodemus into the discussion? Would he ask, "Do you mean, Lord, I need to enter my mother's womb the second time to be born again, then believe in You after my second birth?" Most proponents of this blasphemous teaching belong to the hyper-Calvinist's camp.

But how is it so objectionable when Scriptures are backing this teaching?

John 6:44, for example, acts as the extreme Calvinists'

---

[27] Samson, John. Miscellaneous Quotes (7). Effectualgrace.com. https://effectualgrace.com/2011/01/30/miscellaneous-quotes-7/ (accessed June 14, 2020).

champion verse. From this Scripture, Christ taught that "No one can come to Me unless the Father who sent Me draws him; and I will raise him up on the last day."

It is where the **"born again first before believing"** doctrine got its foothold. The "Father who sent Me draws him." Or God's "Irresistible Grace" (one of the so-called five points) saves you before the foundation of the world, even before trusting Christ. This teaching is unscriptural even if Spurgeon, MacArthur, Sproul, Piper, et al. seem to endorse it!

The Hyper Calvinist's Heresy Qualifies as a Grave False Teaching

The **"Born Again to Believe"** precept is not biblical since you can resist the Father's "drawing you" or His purported "irresistible grace." When the preacher convicted your heart by his sermon, it was the Holy Spirit convicting you and drawing you to Christ. It happened, for example, when Peter preached one sermon which convicted three thousand souls during Pentecost. God drew the Jews to trust Jesus. Now, who can resist our Sovereign God drawing you to the Savior?

Arthur W. Pink, a staunch hyper-Calvinist, defined God as "the Most High, Lord of heaven and earth. Subject to none, influenced by none, absolutely independent; God does as He pleases, only as He pleases, always as He pleases."[28] This faith statement just empowered the hyper-Calvinists' "Irresistible Grace" teaching. If God draws you to believe in Jesus, you cannot resist Him because He said (as quoted by Pink), "My counsel shall stand, and I will do all My pleasure" (Isa 46:10). The **born again first, believe later** teaching got validated

---

28 Arthur W. Pink Quotes. goodreads.com. https://www.goodreads.com/author/quotes/59333.Arthur_W_Pi nk?page=7 (accessed May 31, 2020).

from this contention. But is it biblical? The answer is, No!

Although God is sovereign, He created man as a free moral agent, hence the divine test which forbade Adam and Eve from their continued paradisal occupancy. True, God does as He pleases, but He also said, "Come now, and let us reason together." (Is. 1:18) In Deuteronomy 30, God also required the Israelites binary choices like "life and prosperity, and death and adversity. . .. I have set before you life and death, the blessing and the curse. So choose life." (Vv. 15-20) We cannot interpret the Bible from one side and reject the other truth.

Let's go to Matthew 23. For it is one indisputable Scripture which counters "irresistible grace." Jesus said, "Jerusalem, Jerusalem, who kills the prophets and stones those who are sent to her! How often I wanted to gather your children together, the way a hen gathers her chicks under her wings, and you were unwilling." (v. 37) The Jews rejected God's grace. This verse alone invigorates our thesis that faith in Christ produces the born-again experience and that the "**born again to believe**" teaching is heretical. Christ wanted to save the Jews, but they were resisting God's grace.

The Hyper-Calvinist's Heresy Distorts Man's Depraved Nature

I watched John Piper's sermon on YouTube about Christ's born again teaching and found his thesis anchored on man's **total depravity**. (It is another point of the Calvinist's five points!) One dictionary, the Miriam-Webster says it is "a state of corruption due to original sin held in Calvinism to infect every part of man's nature and to make the natural man unable to know or obey God." The other terms used (to give us a full view of this teaching) are "total inability," "righteous incapability," "radical corruption," and "moral inability." God's rescue of the chosen few from hell without man's free will or freedom to believe in his Savior sums up the Calvinists' bottom line.

The hyper-Calvinists shield their total depravity teaching with dozens of verses from the Scripture. For example, the natural man rejects the Gospel and calls it "foolishness" (1 Cor. 1:18). He cannot understand the things of God (1 Cor. 2:14); he is hostile towards God (Rom. 8:7); dead in transgressions (Eph. 2:5); born in transgression and sin (Ps. 51:5). Man loves the darkness (John 3:19) and sin pleases him (James 1:14-15). Wrote the apostle Paul in Romans chapter three: "There is none righteous, not even one; There is none who understands, There is none who seeks for God." (Vv. 10-11)

John Piper said, "Something we must do, but it is done for us."[29] That is why Peter said that God's "great mercy has caused us to be born again" (1 Pet. 1:3) . . . "who were born, not of blood nor of the will of the flesh nor of the will of man, but of God." (John 1:13) Piper hammered on "God *caused* us to be born again," thus hinting at the **born-again-to-believe** doctrine.

From the same chapter one of First Peter which Piper quoted, we find in verse 23 that the born-again experience happened "not of seed which is perishable but imperishable, that is, through the living and enduring word of God." This Scripture correlates to Paul's getting hold of faith "from hearing, and hearing by the word of Christ." (Rom. 10:17) The second birth, therefore—contrary to the extreme Calvinists' teaching—involves the human free will since it involves faith in Christ and faith requires hearing of the Word which in turn

---

[29] Piper, John. What Happens in the New Birth? Desiringgod.org. https://www.desiringgod.org/messages/what-happens-in-the-new-birth-part-1 (accessed May 31, 2020).

requires the operation of free will.

A little backward glance. Is it the teaching of the Scriptures that the privileged few called the chosen ones do not have the freedom of the will and will enter eternal life like robots since God predestined them to live forever—even against their will? Or that faith in Jesus happens AFTER the born again phenomenon?

"There is a common misconception," wrote gotquestions.com[30], "regarding total depravity. Total depravity does not mean that man is as wicked or sinful as he could be, nor does it mean that man is without a conscience or any sense of right or wrong . . .. It does not even mean that man cannot do things that seem to conform outwardly to the law of God. What the Bible does teach and what total depravity does recognize is that even the "good" things man does are tainted by sin because they are not done for the glory of God and out of faith in Him (Romans 14:23; Hebrews 11:6)."

Observe the two verses just mentioned:

"But he who doubts is condemned if he eats, because his eating is not from faith; and whatever is not from faith is sin. (Rom. 14:23) And without faith it is impossible to please Him, for he who comes to God must believe that He is and that He is a rewarder of those who seek Him." (Heb. 11:6)

It is important to note from the two Scriptures mentioned above that FAITH answers to the hyper-Calvinists' hype on man's depraved nature. Second, faith exists only on the soil of free will. Without freedom, your faith is just rammed down

---

[30] Total depravity - is it biblical? Gotquestions.org. https://www.gotquestions.org/total-depravity.html (accessed May 31, 2020).

your throat. But faith under pressure becomes brainwashing.

Let's have a rundown of our points. Total depravity does not mean complete deletion of the God-wired image of God in man during the fall. "For a man ought not to have his head covered, since he is the IMAGE and GLORY of God." (1 Cor. 11:7) The IMAGE OF GOD in us remains except it is marred by sin.

A space for the church site is always a part of all communities. When religion is suppressed, as with North Korea, the government would invent its own to supply man's hunger for a god. Idols were invented because he desires to worship Someone Bigger.

Let's examine Paul's exhortation that the reality of God is so alive in man's heart:

"For the wrath of God is revealed from heaven against all ungodliness and unrighteousness of men who suppress the truth in unrighteousness, **BECAUSE THAT WHICH IS KNOWN ABOUT GOD IS EVIDENT WITHIN THEM;** for God made it evident to them. For since the creation of the world His invisible attributes, His eternal power and divine nature, have been **CLEARLY SEEN**, being understood through what has been made, so **THAT THEY ARE WITHOUT EXCUSE.** For even though **THEY KNEW GOD,** they **DID NOT HONOR HIM AS GOD** or give thanks, but they became futile in their speculations, and their foolish heart was darkened. Professing to be wise, **THEY BECAME FOOLS,** and **EXCHANGED THE GLORY OF THE INCORRUPTIBLE GOD** for an image in the form of corruptible man and of birds and four-footed animals and crawling creatures." (Rom. 1:18-23)

True, we are depraved. The Thief on the cross was a murderer (and a rapist too). He was more depraved and twisted than us. But Jesus saved him and brought him to Paradise. Why? Because the Thief believed and said, "Jesus, remember me when You come in Your kingdom!"

Jesus replied, "Truly I say to you, today you shall be with Me in Paradise." (Luke 23:42-43)

The hyper-Calvinists would say, God predestined the Thief to eternal life before the world began. The context of this dialog, however, was the rejection of the lost thief. But the other one said, "Jesus, remember me. . ." What faith is it, for Jesus was dying just like him? Yet he believed Jesus would be King of His kingdom, and no death can overpower Him. "Jesus, remember me."

Total depravity is not a complete pull out of the principle and reality of God in man, as evidenced by the snowballing of the cults, the mosques—even surpassing the number of Christian churches!

The Hyper-Calvinist's Heresy Twists God's Command to Repent

The word "repent" floods both the Old and New Testaments because man can repent. For the hyper-Calvinists, however, repentance happens because God helps the chosen person to repent. The free will to repent is missing in their Theology!

What is repentance? In Acts 26:20, Paul said: "that they should repent and turn to God, performing deeds appropriate to repentance." It means it is more than a turning to God (and a turning away from sin) but a change of mind toward God, the Lord Jesus, the Holy Bible, and toward sin. Second, it is connected to bearing "fruit in keeping with repentance." (Matt. 3:8) After Peter repented, he died a martyr's death, never denying Christ again. When Saul repented, he followed Jesus and became the apostle Paul—the man who left all his worldly possessions just to serve our Lord.

In my experience, I learned to love Christ and His Word and changed my old ways after I repented. The constant assault of my anxieties left me as the light of Jesus conquered my soul. Praying to Christ became second nature to me, and the desire to serve Him had gladdened my soul.

Repentance and faith are two sides of the same coin. Said Paul: "I have had one message for Jews and Greeks alike—the necessity of repenting from sin and turning to God, and of having faith in our Lord Jesus." (Acts 20:21, NLT) As faith requires the operation of free will, so is repentance.

The hyper-Calvinists erred in pointing out that genuine repentance is possible outside of the freedom to turn to God and to change one's mind toward the Lord.

A promiscuous husband, for example, who repented for fear of his wife has not repented at all and would recommit his crime at an opportune time. Free will always works with real repentance.

Some governments released their prisoners during the COVID-19 pandemic. Without free will and self-appreciation of their release, most of them consummated the same crime after a week or two. Wrote Mary Wollstonecraft: "Convince a man against his will, He's of the same opinion still."

In Luke 13, some people told Jesus about the government's death penalty where Pilate mixed with their sacrifices the blood of a few Galileans. Responding to it, Christ said it is immaterial in heaven unless you repent.

In this instance, Christ underscored repentance as something attainable. Note Luke 13:1-5:

> "Now on the same occasion there were some present who reported to Him about the Galileans whose blood Pilate had mixed with their sacrifices. And Jesus said to them, 'Do you

suppose that these Galileans were greater sinners than all other Galileans because they suffered this fate? I tell you, no, but unless you repent, you will all likewise perish. Or do you suppose that those eighteen on whom the tower in Siloam fell and killed them were worse culprits than all the men who live in Jerusalem? I tell you, no, but unless you repent, you will all likewise perish.'"

Repentance, from the above Scripture, is taught as man's responsibility since it is within the sphere of his capability.

The **born again to believe** doctrine teaches no repentance at all as the other half of faith since the hyper-Calvinists lead us to believe that God will repent for us.

It is a false doctrine.

The Hyper-Calvinist's Heresy Violates Our Freedom to Believe

The **Born Again to Believe** heresy is a violation of the principle of human free will, because God requires us to believe in Christ to live forever. "Born Again" means salvation or eternal life and no spiritual rebirth until one repents and believes in Christ. Note the famous John 3:16, for it says that "whoever believes in Him [Christ] shall not perish, but have eternal life." Salvation always follows faith. "Believe in the Lord Jesus, and you will be saved." (Acts 16:31) Both repentance and faith exist only in the parameter of freedom. If you are a husband forced by your wife to repent and believe in Jesus, then yours is a fake Christianity. For faith cannot flourish from coercion.

Let us invent a fable of two friends inside the church. "Why are you in the church today?" asked a friend. "Well, my mother told me to attend church because today is my birthday." When the human free will is removed from the core of faith, then that faith is dead and could not stand on its own. In Romans 10, the apostle Paul wrote about how human free will work as regards calling or believing in our Lord. He said in verse 13: "Whoever will call on the name of the Lord will be saved." And in verse 17: "So faith comes from hearing, and hearing by the word of Christ."

Both "calling" and "hearing" are action words requiring freedom of the will.

The **Born Again to Believe** doctrine dismisses that essential element known as the human free will. It is predestination, but God requires His children to love Him under the climate of freedom. We must believe after hearing the Word of Christ (not under compulsion by an Irresistible Grace!)—or believe to be born again. It is what the Bible teaches. Believe to be born again!

The Hyper-Calvinist's Heresy Babbles on Hard Determinism

From YouTube and other sources, we can gather tons of information about the **born again to believe** theology. To understand this heresy, we need to examine the hyper-Calvinists' possession of God's foreknowledge and hard determinism.

Let's explore Isaiah 46 since most Calvinists hire this chapter in their understanding of God. From verse nine to eleven, God said,

> "For I am God, and there is no other; I am God, and there is no one like Me, Declaring the end from the beginning, And from ancient times things which have not been done, Saying, 'My purpose will be established, And I will accomplish all My good pleasure' . . . Truly I have spoken; truly I will bring it to pass. I have planned it, surely I will do it." (Is. 46:9-11b)

John Piper, one of the most prominent hyper-Calvinists in this generation, understands this Scripture as God's hard determinism. He planned everything (including your salvation), and will surely do it. I watched a YouTube presentation of Piper saying Christ as God knew Peter would deny Him and Judas would orchestrate His crucifixion. We believe God knows everything, but it is unscriptural to teach that God is involved in Judas' rebellious mind. God did not plan that Hitler would kill six million Jews. God is not a party to sin. He does not plant unrighteousness into man's heart. Otherwise, He would become the God of unrighteousness.

Second, if God predestined people to hell, then He would become unjust for sending billions to hell on things not their fault.

The apostle Paul wrote that "[T]he wrath of God is revealed from heaven against all ungodliness and unrighteousness of men who suppress the truth in unrighteousness." (Rom. 1:18) While the man is wicked, God is holy and perfect, and He could not have planned and carried out (as Piper argued) all the surrounding murders. It is just absurd. Man is very sinful deep inside him. He suppresses God's truth in unrighteousness. "The heart is more deceitful than all else And is desperately sick." (Jer. 17:9a) And his conscience knows it, "so that they are without excuse." (Rom. 1:20b) He has the light of Christ because Jesus enlightens every man. (John 1:9)

A pastor friend told me he was against hyper-Calvinism until he met Acts 13:48, which states that "as many as had been appointed to eternal life believed." **Born again to believe**?

The best commenters on Acts 13:48 suggest the phrase, "As many as were DISPOSED for eternal life believed" (Read:

Benson Commentary[31]). They have reasons we can Google, but I like the comment from the "Expositor's Greek Testament" which says verse 46 solves the Calvinistic hint of the verse. It says: "Paul and Barnabas spoke out boldly and said, 'It was necessary that the word of God be spoken to you first; since you repudiate it and judge yourselves unworthy of eternal life, behold, we are turning to the Gentiles.'" (Acts 13:46)

Look, the Israelites were preordained to eternal life, but they rejected the Gospel, so "we are turning to the Gentiles." This proves that verse 48 does not mean all the Gentiles in that preaching got salvation, without first believing. It is theologically slanted to say the Israelites got a societal condemnation, and the Gentiles, group salvation or eternal life. The word "disposed" here makes more sense than "appointed" or "ordained."

Note Acts 13:48 from NASB:

"When the Gentiles heard this, they began rejoicing and glorifying the word of the Lord; and as many as had been appointed to eternal life believed."

Meyer's NT Commentary[32] said that the conception of an absolute decree (appointed to eternal life) does not exclude individual freedom.

Ravi Zacharias once said that a truth claim invalidates determinism. If we believe that God predetermines our future, then it is a truth claim from the bare bones of free will. God offers us free salvation by faith in Christ. But if you cannot accept it, your choice to reject our Lord (your truth claim)

---

[31] https://biblehub.com/commentaries/acts/13-48.htm (accessed May 31, 2020).

[32] Ibid.

invalidates God's hard determinism. Our freedom of choice is a scriptural teaching, and we cannot suppress it by promoting the Scriptures used to advance predestination.

Most extreme Calvinists, for example, celebrate Romans 9:13 as their shielding verse. It says, "Just as it is written, 'Jacob I loved, but Esau I hated.'" Malachi, in discussing this truth, spoke about posterity. In verse three of chapter one, Malachi wrote: "but I have hated Esau, and I have made his mountains a desolation and appointed his inheritance for the jackals of the wilderness." Does it mean to say all the descendants of Esau were damned, and Jacob's saved? Clear. It is not about predestination. It is about God's honoring His covenant with Abraham. In the New Testament, Paul wrote: "Therefore, be sure that it is those who are of faith who are sons of Abraham." (Gal. 3:7) Faith in Jesus is required to get salvation, but something is needed, which is to hear the Word. "So faith comes from hearing, and hearing by the word of Christ." (Rom. 10:17) In these issues, human free will always make sense since you don't hear the Word by asking God (in the name of grace) to hear it for you.

14. THE FUTURE OF THE BORN-AGAIN CHRISTIAN

And inasmuch as it is appointed for men to die once and after this comes judgment. — Hebrews 9:27.

I WANT TO share the story of Dr. W. Herschel Ford. One night, recalled Dr. Ford, a young preacher preached on Hebrews 9:27. A highly intelligent unbeliever returned in the morning and grilled the pastor with hard questions the latter couldn't answer. Playing safe, the pastor just used his text to answer all questions: "And inasmuch as it is appointed for men to die once and after this comes judgment." Long story short, the text hounded the man as he couldn't put it down. So he visited the pastor again. "True, I am a sinner," said the man. "I am lost. I know it is appointed for me to die and then the judgment. Tell me right now how to be saved."[33]

Commented Ford, "Men go up and down the streets, ignoring the church, forgetting God, chasing the pleasures of this world, filling the bars and places of sin, ignoring this one great fact, 'It is appointed unto men once to die.'"[34] I may add, "And then the judgment."

I heard people commenting they don't appreciate sermons on death and judgment. But we will all die. We need to prepare for God's judgment, for after death "comes judgment."

Wrote J. C. Ryle that we have an undying soul:

"The world is not all. The life that we have now live in the flesh is

---

[33] W. Herschel Ford, Simple Sermons on Heaven, Hell, and Judgment (Zondervan Publishing House, Grand Rapids Michigan, 1969), pp. 84-89.

[34] Ibid.

not the only life. There is a life to come. We have souls . . . Let us establish it in our minds as a great fact, that we all carry within our bosoms something that will never die. This body of ours, which takes up so much of our thoughts and time, to warm it, dress it, feed it, and make it comfortable, — this body alone is not all the man. It is but the lodging of a noble tenant, and that tenant is the immortal soul!"[35]

Without salvation from sin, the undying soul will be tormented in hell forever. Some said fire consumes things, therefore, the unsaved soul will be annihilated in the lake of fire. The Annihilationist also argues that man's sin in time cannot be punished in eternity. To take down doubts, however, the Bible taught that God would cast the unbelievers into the lake of fire which would also torment Satan, the devil. If it were a prison cell, God would send the unforgiven soul to the devil's black hole. And this place called "lake of fire" does a day-and-night job of tormenting all those sent to it. Revelation 20 states that,

> ". . .the devil who deceived them was thrown into the lake of fire and brimstone, where the beast and the false prophet are also; and they will be tormented day and night forever and ever." (v. 10)

The salvation of the soul is all we have on this planet. My entire life of study about eternal life and God is not enough remuneration when heaven opens for me at the end of my journey.

We need Jesus for our assurance of immortal bliss. If I have a brain the size of the world, I will fill each cell with faith in Jesus. The value of my soul is all that matters, and only Christ can give me eternal life in Paradise.

Hell is never an option after this sojourn.

---

[35] J. C. Ryle, Old Paths (The Banner of Truth Trust, Edinburgh,U.K., First Published, 1878, Reprinted 2005), pp. 41-42.

The Born-Again Christian and the Appointment for a Judgment After Death

We have a soul! Our appointment with God for judgment will take place, even if we don't believe it. We don't have other business after death, but to face God's judgment.

Spurgeon once said that "Great numbers of persons have no concern about eternal things. They care more about their cats and dogs than about their souls . . . .. This is great foolishness . . . when death is so near, and judgment is so sure."[36]

Since the born-again Christian is a saved child of God, he won't stand together with the infidels before our Almighty Father for the judgment of the unbelievers. Christ's rejecters will be judged on the grounds of their unforgiven sins, but those born of God's Spirit "have redemption through [Christ's] blood, the forgiveness of sins, according to the riches of his grace." (Eph. 1:7) Christ also taught that "he who hears My word, and believes Him who sent Me, has eternal life, and DOES NOT COME INTO JUDGMENT, but has passed out of death into life." (John 5:24)

Wrote Henry C. Thiessen:

The believer in Christ is accordingly freed from the guilt and penalty of sin, because Christ has accepted the guilt and paid the penalty for him. No believer will be judged for his sins, since he has been judged for them already in Christ (John 5:24). There is however, a present judgment for believers. It is the judgment of sin in their own life. Paul admonishes believers to judge themselves in private (1 Cor. 11:31f.) and in

---

[36] C. H. Spurgeon. The Spurgeon Archive (Around the Wicket Gate). https://archive.spurgeon.org/misc/wg.php (accessed January 1, 2021)

church life (1 Cor. 5:5; 1 Tim. 1:20; 5:19f.). The Lord chastens his disobedient children in order to induce them to judge and put away sins out of their lives (2 Sam. 7:14f, 12:13f.; Heb. 12:5-13)."[37]

The judgment of sin happened at the cross of Christ over 2000 years ago. But the blood of Jesus cannot cleanse the soul of the unbelievers. In Matthew 26, Christ said, "for this is My blood of the covenant, which is poured out for many for forgiveness of sins." The phrase, "for many" affirms that His sacrifice on the cross redeems not everyone but the believers only. Paul taught that our redemption is in Christ Jesus "whom God displayed publicly as a propitiation in His blood through FAITH, so that He would be just and the justifier of the one who has FAITH in Jesus." (Rom. 3:24-26) Without FAITH, the rejecters of our Lord will face God's wrath and His righteous judgment after their death.

At the end of this life, the soul of the born-again Christian will live with God. That said, the apostle Paul desired to depart (or to die) and be with Christ, "for that is very much better." (Phil. 1:23) Our souls in heaven would be better off than our existence on the earth today, even before the giving of our spiritual bodies, which would happen during the Rapture.

Is there no judgment for the born-again Christians aside from God's chastisement in many forms for the sin committed? Or let's talk about self-judgment, mental anguish, and the conviction by the Holy Spirit for disobeying the Lord? Well, we must present ourselves at the Judgment Seat of Christ. Wrote Paul:

---

[37]Henry C. Thiessen, Lectures in Systematic Theology (Wm. B. Eerdmans Publishing Company, Grand Rapids, MI, Copyright 1979; Reprint, Philippines: The Christian Library Inc., 1991), pp. 389-392.

"For we must all appear before the judgment seat of Christ, so that each one may be recompensed for his deeds in the body, according to what he has done, whether good or bad." (2 Cor. 5:10)

The word "we" in this Scripture includes Paul, the author, in this judgment. Based on its context, we find it as the believers' accounting of their lives to Christ. "So then each one of us will give an account of himself to God." (Rom. 14:10) Henry Thiessen wrote that "The believer will be judged to ascertain whether he is eligible for a reward or not, and if so, how large that reward is to be (1 Cor. 3:12-15). It is clear that the Lord will call his servants to himself for a private judgment of their works (Luke 19:15; 2 Cor. 5:10)."[38]

In the "Parable of Money Usage," Christ said, "When he returned, after receiving the kingdom, he ordered that these slaves, to whom he had given the money, be called to him so that he might know what business they had done." (Luke 19:15) It is the point in the Judgment Seat: "What have I done for Jesus?" It is the giving of rewards, not proclamation of eternal damnation as with those haters of Jesus in the White Throne Judgment.

The Born-Again Christian and His Resurrection

After his death, the born-again believer will go straight to our Father's home to join with Jesus and the angels of God in heaven. During the Rapture (or the snatching away of the living believers to meet Jesus in the air) the souls of the dead believers in heaven will reunite with their resurrected bodies. In short, the resurrection of the dead believers would occur during the Rapture. The living born-again Christians would be given new spiritual bodies. "For the Lord Himself will descend

---

[38] Ibid. Thiessen. P. 375.

from heaven with a shout, with the voice of the archangel and with the trumpet of God, and the dead in Christ will rise first. Then we who are alive and remain will be caught up together with them in the clouds to meet the Lord in the air, and so we shall always be with the Lord." (1 Thess. 4:16-17)

The apostle Paul clarified that "in a moment, in the twinkling of an eye, at the last trumpet; for the trumpet will sound, and the dead will be raised imperishable, and we will be changed." It is the resurrection of the born-again believers only since the Apostle thanked God "who gives us the victory through our Lord Jesus Christ." (1 Cor. 15:52, 57)

Arthur E. Bloomfield summarizes the resurrection and the rapture in the following:

> "The Rapture. (Luke 17:34-37; 1 Cor. 15:51-52; 1 Thess. 4:16, 17; Dan. 12:1-3; Rev. 4:1, 2; Rev. 12:5). There is no difference between Resurrection and Rapture except that the one refers to those who are dead, and the other to those who are living. If all the dead in Christ will be raised, then all the living in Christ will be caught up. The purpose of the Resurrection and Rapture is to clothe the saved with their immortal bodies. It is the beginning of immortality. It is timed so that the living in Christ may escape the tribulation."[39]

God will also resurrect the dead unbelievers in Hades, but only after the Millennium for the White Throne Judgment. It is the casting out of the billions of non-regenerated peoples on the earth to the lake of fire. The doctrine of Christ in Matthew 10 then becomes crystal clear: "Do not fear those who kill the body but are unable to kill the soul; but rather fear Him who

---

[39] Bloomfield, Arthur E. Before the Last Battle: Armageddon. Minneapolis, Minn., Bethany House, 1999. P. 45.

is able to destroy both soul and body in hell." (v. 28) The destruction of the unsaved soul with his resurrected body implies eternal torment in the fires of God's wrath.

It is a horrifying truth for the Bible believers since our Lord affirms this fact. He said in Matthew 16: "For what will it profit a man if he gains the whole world and forfeits his soul? Or what will a man give in exchange for his soul?" (v. 26)

From the time I trusted the Holy Bible as the Word of God, I always felt goosebumps as I thought about my unsaved loved ones wallowing (body and soul!) in Christ's version of hell forever without a savior.

The infidels won't care about hell and our fears for their eternal damnation. But their unbelief cannot alter this Gospel truth. God said, "But for the cowardly and unbelieving and abominable and murderers and immoral persons and sorcerers and idolaters and all liars, their part will be in the lake that burns with fire and brimstone, which is the second death." The unbelievers are not afraid of the second death. God loves them too, but He cannot save them until they repent and believe in Jesus!

While the souls of the dead believers are awaiting their resurrection at the Rapture, the hopeless unbelievers would suffer the torments in Hades. Then, after the Millennium, they would resurrect for their final judgment in the lake of fire forever. It is the White Throne Judgment. It will be the fulfillment of Daniel 12:2: "Many of those who sleep in the dust of the ground will awake, these to everlasting life, but the others to disgrace and everlasting contempt."

Social media is like a pool of both stupidities and intellectualism vying for the reader's attention. However, non-Christians waste their time on Facebook for the things of this world only. The followers of Christ are different since each born-again Christian will be given a spiritual body during the

Rapture. It carries weight for them. Then Christ will fulfill His promise:

> "I will not leave you as orphans; I will come to you. After a little while the world will no longer see Me, but you will see Me; because I live, you will live also. In that day you will know that I am in My Father, and you in Me, and I in you." (John 14:18-20)

The apostle John said, "we will be like Him." (1 John 3:2b) We would have a resurrected body like Jesus!

The Born-Again Christian and the Things to Come

We discussed in Chapter Eleven the saved Christians' assurance of salvation. From this truth, we can see the future from the landscape of safety. The pretribulation Rapture of the church gathers more support as we are not appointed to suffer the wrath of God. In Second Thessalonians 5:9, Paul said, "God has not destined us for wrath, but for obtaining salvation through our Lord Jesus Christ."

The Wrath of God

God's wrath is our Father's righteous anger on those haters of the truth. Paul said, "For the wrath of God is revealed from heaven against all ungodliness and unrighteousness of men who suppress the truth in unrighteousness, because that which is known about God is evident within them; for God made it evident to them." (Rom. 1:18-19) The truth that God created all things is incontestable since no one scientist can ever produce soil out of nothing as what God did in creating the world. The biblical teaching is that Jesus Himself is the WAY, the TRUTH, and the LIFE. (John 14:6) But leaders in academia push for evolution instead of God's creation. They are suppressing the truth in unrighteousness. Is it not a mark of revolting unrighteousness when you attribute every mystery of the order in the solar system as the work of nature, and not of God? Another instance of unrighteousness that provokes God's wrath is the suppression of the universal law of gender. God populated the world, including the animal kingdom, through the male and female union. To suppress this truth, many invented hundreds of genders to sedate their consciences for their shameless and perverted sexual behavior. The danger is God's implanting the sword of His wrath on all those suppressing the truth in unrighteousness.

Those having no born-again experience will suffer the wrath of God in this life and in the age to come. God's wrath in this life translates into the lack of peace with God; the absence of hope for immortality; and the fear of death. These hell-induced symptoms will culminate with the soul's torments and "gnashing of teeth" in Hades, and finally, in the lake of fire. By its bottom line, sin makes man naturally disdainful for the things related to the wrath of God.

The Great Tribulation

During the Tribulation, God's wrath will be mixed with grace since multitudes will be saved at this period. After three and a half years of divine preaching, those killed for the name of Christ would be resurrected to compose the throng of the Tribulation Saints. The Old Testament Saints, according to Bloomfield, would be resurrected at the end of the first half of the Tribulation, but some said it would happen at the end. Whichever, we consider them a part of the First Resurrection.

The born-again Christians, the Tribulation and the Old Testament Saints (called the saints, bondservants or armies (Rev. 19:14)) would accompany Christ at His Second Coming after the Rapture. He would defeat all His enemies (Satan and the armies of the nations) at the Battle of Armageddon. (Rev. 19:11-16) Then the Millennial Age would begin which is also the establishment of Christ's Eternal Kingdom on the earth with the saints (of which the born-again Christians will be one of them!) serving as the administrators and priests of God. (Luke 19:17; Rev. 1:6, KJV; 1 Pet. 2:9; Is. 61:6) They will reign with Christ forever and ever (Rev. 22:5) while lodging at the New Jerusalem suspended above the earth. From it, John 14:3 finds its fulfillment: "If I go and prepare a place for you, I will come again and receive you to Myself, that where I am, there you may be also."

The Rapture and the Resurrection

Pretribulational Rapture is Christ's meeting the living and dead born-again Christians in the air before the Tribulation Period. (1 Thess. 4:17) The dead will be resurrected, and the living changed to a spiritual body. It is about the resurrection of the believers, to simplify our mental picture of it, according to Bloomfield. It is the first event of Christ's Second Coming. His feet won't touch the earth yet. Said Paul,

> "For the Lord Himself will descend from heaven with a shout, with the voice of the archangel and with the trumpet of God, and the dead in Christ will rise first. Then we who are alive and remain will be caught up together with them in the clouds to meet the Lord in the air, and so we shall always be with the Lord." (1 Thess. 4:16-17)

Pretribulationism (or pre-wrath) gathers more acceptance than Midtribulationism or Posttribulationism since the Lord will return "like a thief in the night." (2 Thess. 5:2)

During the Rapture, the Lord will snatch away His followers from all walks of life in a wink of an eye. This great event would hit the world into tragedies as when the born-again pilot or surgeon would disappear miraculously in the middle of his task. The Laodicean churches would continue their services, and those hoping to enter heaven by their self-righteousness would remember this Christian doctrine about the Rapture. The first half of the Tribulation would follow the Rapture. Many will repent and trust Christ during this time.

The Bondservants of the Lord

The kingdom of Christ on earth "will have no end." It is staying forever. All those partakers of the First Resurrection (the born-again Christians, the Tribulation, and the Old Testament saints) will become Christ's "bondservants" who will serve Him forever in the administration of His kingdom. Wrote the apostle John:

> "The rest of the dead did not come to life until the thousand years were completed. This is the first resurrection. Blessed and holy is the one who has a part in the first resurrection; over these the second death has no power, but they will be PRIESTS OF GOD and of Christ and WILL REIGN WITH HIM for a thousand years . . .. There will no longer be any curse; and the throne of God and of the Lamb will be in it, and His BOND-SERVANTS WILL SERVE HIM; they will see His face, and His name will be on their foreheads. And there will no longer be any night; and they will not have need of the light of a lamp nor the light of the sun, because the Lord God will illumine them; and they WILL REIGN FOREVER AND EVER." (Rev. 20:5-6; 22:3-5)

It is the meaning of Luke 19:17: "And he said to him, 'Well done, good slave, because you have been faithful in a very little thing, you are to be in authority over ten cities.'"

Some saved people in heaven will have a rank higher than others based on their service to Christ today. (Rev. 19:5) Will the mega-church pastors occupy a higher position in heaven?

The best answer is, "We don't know." Our Lord, however, taught that "whoever wishes to become great among you shall be your servant, and whoever wishes to be first among you shall be your slave; just as the Son of Man did not come to be served, but to serve, and to give His life a ransom for many." (Matt. 20:26-28)

Christ's Earthly Kingdom

The Rapture precedes the 7-year Tribulation Period. This whole process is related to the establishment of Christ's kingdom on the earth for a thousand years, the period attributed to the perfection of His eternal kingdom in this world. After the Millennium, Christ's Kingdom will assume perfection and will come to its eternal state. The complete burning-of-the-earth doctrine in the last days, therefore, is false because Christ will set up His kingdom here forever, and not on another planet. (2 Peter 3:10)

Angel Gabriel, for proof, said to Mary:

"And behold, you will conceive in your womb and bear a son, and you shall name Him Jesus. He will be great and will be called the Son of the Most High; and the Lord God will give Him the throne of His father David; and HE WILL REIGN OVER THE HOUSE OF JACOB FOREVER, and HIS KINGDOM WILL HAVE NO END." (Luke 1:33-34)

The apostle Paul talked about three kinds of people. He said, "Give no offense either to Jews or to Greeks or to the church of God." (1 Cor. 10:32) We can trim this Scripture as the Chosen People (the Jewish Nation); the Greeks (or the Gentile Nations); and the Church or all those partakers (the Tribulation and the Old Testament Saints included) of the First Resurrection. These three groups will be on the earth during the Millennium, *(1)* the Jewish Nation will serve as the nucleus of the kingdom ("the house of Jacob"—Luke 1:33-34); *(2)* the Gentiles, the people or subjects in the kingdom (called the Nations. See Rev. 21:24-26); and *(3)* the resurrected born-again Christians and the other saints will be there to rule or reign with Christ (Rev. 2:26-27) from the Holy City, the New Jerusalem.

All the First Resurrection saints will have immortal bodies. Daniel 7:27 would become more unambiguous: *"Then the sovereignty, the dominion and the greatness of all the kingdoms under the whole heaven will be given to the people of the saints of the Highest One; His kingdom will be an everlasting kingdom, and all the dominions will serve and obey Him."*[40]

The Jews

Christ will save those unbelieving Jews after their most terrible trials. Wrote Paul:

> And so all Israel will be saved; just as it is written, "The Deliverer will come from Zion, He will remove ungodliness from Jacob. This is My covenant with them, When I take away their sins." (Rom. 11:26-27)

Those dead Jews who were partakers of the First Resurrection will reign with Christ. Those who will remain as earthly people occupying the land promised them will live peacefully with the Gentile nations. They will form the nucleus of the eternal kingdom. God will revive the kingdom of David (See 2 Sam. 7:10,12-13; Luke 1:32,33.), and it will be, to use Bloomfield, "Israelitish." (Cf. Jer. 23:3-8)

The Nations

The unsaved Gentiles who will survive the Great Tribulation will be forced to worship Christ during the Millennium, as they will be ruled with a rod of iron. Otherwise, there will be no rain on them. (See Ps. 2:7-9; Matt. 25:31; Micah 4:1-3; Zech. 14:16-19.) As subjects of the kingdom, their genuine

---

[40] Reference: Arthur E. Bloomfield, Before the Last Battle— Armageddon (Minnesota: Bethany House Publishers, 1971)

unbelief would be tested after the release of Satan for a little while after the Millennium. (Rev. 20:7-10; Matt. 25:31-46)

The merging of the nations with the saints forges a conclusion that God will be "all in all," making all things new and not remembering the old things. The melt-the-earth doctrine follows this narrative. But many other prophecies need fulfillment like the ever-expanding kingdom of our Lord, given the immortality of the earthly people. Observe Isaiah 60:21-22:

"Then all your people will be righteous; They will possess the land forever, The branch of My planting, The work of My hands, That I may be glorified. THE SMALLEST ONE WILL BECOME A CLAN, AND THE LEAST ONE A MIGHTY NATION. I, the Lord, will hasten it in its time." (Isa. 60:21-22) (See also Isa. 45:17-18; Luke 1:31-32, Isa. 9:7; Rev. 22:5; 21:24-26; Dan. 7:27, etc.)

The Earthly People

Wrote Arthur E. Bloomfield:

"Then there will be Gentile nations, made up of those who are saved during the Millennium or who are born during the Millennium and after. They are of the earth. They will not go into the Holy City to live. They will inhabit the earth or the earthly kingdom forever. Everlasting life in that day will not mean that they will die and be raised; it will mean that they will never die. They will remain an earthly people. Their number will increase forever. God is not limited in His power to provide room.

"The saints are a fixed number. They will not increase. They are a distinct people who live in the City of God and see His face. They are the rulers, with Christ, of all creation, heirs of all things, joint-heirs with Christ.

"Redeemed Jews (those who are saved and have become

immortal) are included with the saints. There is no difference because of nationality in the Holy City. Both Old and New Testament saints are there (Rev. 21:12, 14).

"The earthly nation of Israel will be saved as an earthly nation and David will reign. It is the nucleus of the kingdom on earth; Christ and the saints will reign for 1000 years; after that the kingdom will assume its permanent form, with the Jews inhabiting their Promised Land and other nations living in peace with them.

"The new heaven and the new earth mentioned in Revelation 20 are the result of the reign of Christ for 1000 years. 'Old things have passed away, behold, all things have become new. . ..'"

"THE 144,000 ISRAELITES SEALED. These are Jews. They are saved after the Rapture, the same as the Tribulation Saints. But due to the fact that they are in Palestine, over which Antichrist has no power at the time, they are not subject to the persecution suffered by the Gentile converts. They are not killed; therefore, they cannot very well be raised from the dead. They will remain on the earth, the firstfruits of the kingdom of David (Rev. 7:1-8; 14:1-5)."[41]

After the Millennium

Our premise is straightforward. First, God will renovate the earth but not destroy it because it will be inhabited forever. (Isa. 45:17,18) Second, our Lord's kingdom on earth will have no end. (Luke 1:31-32; Isa. 9:7) Third, that earth will be populated by the immortal people, which are the Jewish and the Gentile Nations. Last, the resurrected saints who will have immortal bodies will reign with Christ forever. (Rev. 22:5; 21:24-26; Dan. 7:27)

We have tension with the following biblical thoughts: a)

---

[41] Ibid. Arthur E. Bloomfield. pp. 42; 46.

that all things will pass away; b) no remembrance to all things; c) the earth will melt by intense heat; d) "then comes the end," etc. How do we reconcile them?

Well, tears and death will pass away, but not the earth and the soul. Second, in the Parable of the Rich Man and Lazarus, the rich man remembered. (Luke 19:25) We would not have Alzheimer's, but perfection in heaven. Third, the "intense heat" is about the redemption and cleansing of the earth. If you advocate the melting of the earth as equivalent to destroying it, then where shall you place these ever-increasing people, each one of whom will become a mighty nation?

As born-again Christians, God fastens our final state to the work of ruling and judging the earthly people. We will have immortal bodies as heirs and children of God in Christ, our beloved Savior. First Peter 1:9-10 now makes more sense:

> "But you are a chosen race, a royal priesthood, a holy nation, a people for God's own possession, so that you may proclaim the excellencies of Him who has called you out of darkness into His marvelous light; for you once were not a people, but now you are the people of God; you had not received mercy, but now you have received mercy."

The born-again Christians are the chosen race (including all those partakers of the First Resurrection!) for God's own possession. He would resurrect us and give us immortal bodies since He is not the God of the dead—since He would not have the dry bones for His own possession! Then He would assign us to rule and judge in Christ's eternal kingdom. Can we not praise God for such a sunny and golden eternal future because of our faith in the substitutionary death of our dear Savior, Jesus Christ?

15. CONCLUSION

*"Behold, now is 'THE ACCEPTABLE TIME,'
behold, now is 'THE DAY OF SALVATION.'" — 2
Corinthians 6:2.*

ALL ETERNAL BLESSINGS emanate from this far-reaching doctrine of the second birth. It is the "hinge of the gospel," Spurgeon said. Unless one is born again, he cannot see the kingdom of God.

Our assurance of heaven is more imperative when we understand the unpredictability of death. Let us not live life unprepared like most of our friends. One prominent politician, for example, bragged that she licked away her cancer in three months. She died in her sleep a few months after her televised announcement. Unprepared!

Atheistic Intellectualism Hinders a Man from Having the Born-Again Experience

The Internet provides us with everything we need to know about the rejecters' common objections against the Christian faith. We cannot tell the totality of the unbelievers' hatred toward Jesus in one sentence. But we can put in a nutshell their shared drive to wage war against the God of the Holy Bible. They hate God. That said, we can look at the nonbelievers empirically from the fabric of Christ's twin teachings that He is the Truth, and that the devil is the father of lies. As we analyzed the infidels' worldviews and hostility toward Bible Christianity, we met nothing more than abhorrence for the truth and their hatred for the God of the Scriptures. "Transgressing and denying the Lord," wrote Isaiah, "And turning away from our God, Speaking oppression and revolt, Conceiving in and uttering from the heart lying words." (59:13)

Paul also said that the unbelievers would "accumulate for themselves teachers in accordance to their own desires." (2 Tim. 4:3) In short, they want to cement and perpetuate their unbelief.

I followed a Facebook page that knocks around the academia's concealment of the ever-growing archaeological finds that could wipe out somehow crucial parts of Darwin's theory of evolution. The pyramids of Egypt, for example, prove the stone-age tools used were more advanced than our present-day superior devices. The mysterious monuments (like the great pyramids, the stone henges, and other megalithic structures) demonstrate the superiority of tools, knowledge, and workmanship. These unexplained facts (thousands of them) tear down Darwinism. Did the Darwinians care that they embrace an erroneous belief or theory?

It is the problem. While the evolutionists don't mind the flaws of Darwin's natural selection, those people questioning the academia attribute their conspiracy theories to aliens and extra-terrestrial beings. Both camps left God out of the equation. They locked horns on things outside of God's truth. To these people, Christ said, "Let them alone; they are blind guides of the blind. And if a blind man guides a blind man, both will fall into a pit." (Matt. 15:14)

All those non-Christians who are interested in the mysteries of the universe were like those drunk campers who woke up at two o'clock in the morning and debated the star formations and the planets without understanding that someone stole their tent. Ravi Zacharias once shared that story of people missing the point.

Famed newly developed technologies and the constant

digging by thousands of archaeologists have uncovered fast the mysterious structures left by the ancient people. But if God were to explain these things, He would connect all to the superpowers of the devil as the fallen angel, Lucifer. Wrote Paul: "For the mystery of lawlessness is already at work; that is, the one whose coming is in accord with the activity of Satan, with all power and signs and false wonders." (2 Thess. 2:7,9)

Let us not miss the point. God gave us life to get salvation from His hell-judgment through faith in Christ. We need not go into details concerning all the riddles embedded with the pyramids of Egypt. It is unnecessary to life's meaning, which is the assurance of our immortality in heaven after death through having the second birth experience.

Wrote the apostle Paul: "For the wisdom of this world is foolishness before God. For it is written, 'He is the one who catches the wise in their craftiness'; and again, "The Lord knows the reasonings of the wise, that they are useless.'" (1 Cor. 3:19-20)

From the websites of the humanists and atheists, we find their familiar protest that the "Bible is full of contradictions and discrepancies; full of violence, genocide, prejudice, and injustice (often commanded by God). The ancient and primitive people wrote the Bible, and has no value to modern people anymore."

Again, it is the problem. These people attack the Bible, the Book of Truth, based on what they see; on what their limited brains can comprehend as if they can put God into their laboratory test tubes.

Ravi Zacharias once shared a story about a proud atheist who supported fanatically the Theory of Evolution. He then asked the guy if the mind or the brain is the product of time + matter + chance—the familiar Darwinian formula for evolution! While listening to Ravi's discussion through YouTube, I realized how foolish and deceived were those intellectuals teaching Darwinism.

Another point raised by the Creationists is the intelligent design and purpose in the material world. The irreducible complexity of the DNA, for example, is one example of a designer, our God, who designed everything in nature and the celestial domain.

For another example, we find that Darwin's Natural Selection theory cannot produce a table, since it requires a carpenter to design and build it.

We find, therefore, that too much intellectualism can hinder a man from experiencing a rebirth. The Bible said we are "always learning and never able to come to the knowledge of the truth." (2 Tim. 3:7)

The central issue is our life after death, and no amount of scholarship and research-based study can surpass the earnestness and solemnity of our hope to live forever by faith in Christ.

One church pastor, for instance, had a father who used to shout lengthy Bible verses before breakfast throughout his life. This man, however, was a church thief. He was church treasurer three times and was kicked out of office three times. He would march his way toward hell, memorizing verses! For though in his head, you will find Christ, in his heart, you will find Judas, the thief.

You can be highly intelligent but unsaved. So, what's the point of your genius, when all you have in the future is endless suffering in the fires of hell?

Salvation is not memory verses or philosophical expertise since all forms of scholarship cannot guarantee eternal life. One can be an unsaved Doctor of Education or Theology!

Too Much Pride Hinders a Man from Having the Born-Again Experience

Pride ranks high in the list of roadblocks on the highway of salvation. After Adam's temptation in Paradise, his self-confidence grew from the devil's promise that his "eyes will be opened, and you will be like God, knowing good and evil. (Gen. 3:5) For example, the woman in Samaria who had five husbands told Christ: "Sir, I perceive that You are a prophet. Our fathers worshiped in this mountain." (John 4:19-20) It was her way of saying, "You've got a Gospel, but we have a religion of our own—in this mountain!" A concealed pride, right? I experienced being told to leave the house because "we've our religion; we've our God." Pride closes the mind to accept Christ's invitation to live forever. It hinders a man from experiencing a rebirth.

Before our Lord, Nicodemus also showed a ray of confidence in his bias as a Pharisee. It prompted Christ to ask: "Are you the teacher of Israel"?

Christ's teaching regarding the second birth is so simple that He calls it gospel or good news. It is good news indeed to be saved and to live forever with God by merely "looking at," or believing in Him. "For this is the will of My Father," taught Christ, "that everyone who BEHOLDS the Son and believes in Him will have eternal life, and I Myself will raise him up on the last day." (John 6:40)

The Gospel, however, hurts man. For it radically dwarfs his natural feelings of self-worth.

In every phase of his life, he wants to feel he is the exclusive star player. But the simplicity of the Gospel insults his innate capabilities to do things his own way. The Gospel cuts a man's pride. May I reiterate the devil's teaching in Eden? His greatest lie continues to fool man today:

"... you will be as gods knowing good and evil" (Gen. 3:5, KJV).

The Gospel hurts man, for he is not ego-involved. After all, he knows—or so he thinks he knows—good and evil!

The concept of the second birth through the sacrifice of Another, that is Christ, is very seriously offensive to his darling pride.

Christ came to die for our sins. But man wants to pay the penalty of his sins by his own self-righteousness; he wants to do things the way he likes because he is so drugged by the devil's spiel: "you will be as gods knowing good and evil."

The Gospel (that Christ died for our sins) irks man, as he cannot flatter himself with it—he cannot save himself under Christ's salvation plan!

Today, all people believe they have the satanic sense of discerning right and wrong. Pride dominates the man. Wrote prophet Isaiah:

For the Lord of hosts will have a day of reckoning
Against everyone who is proud and lofty
And against everyone who is lifted up,
That he may be abased." (Is. 2:12)

From there, Christ said, unless you are born again, you cannot live in God's city. This teaching bites man's ego and self-admiration as a little god with the talent to understand Satan's version of right and wrong. I can imagine Nicodemus' arguing with Christ, and saying, "Lord, according to my Theology, I am sinless, and have never broken a law." But our Lord replied something like this: You need a rebirth, a regeneration, birth by the Spirit of God to enter heaven. It's not about your sincerity in religion, Nicodemus. Rather, it is about your second birth experience through the action of the Spirit of God upon your soul. Everything in your profile as an admirably moral person is useless until you are born again by faith in the Son of God.

An Unreasonable Hesitation Hinders a Man from Having the Born-Again Experience

John R. Rice once said that God presents His plan for our salvation in many terms. For instance, to be born again one may come to Christ, believe or trust in Him, or look at Him in faith.

One afternoon, someone invited me to see a man gasping for breath. His broken words dropped out of his lips so lazily, as if the power of death curbed his tongue and pulled back his speech. He was a member of the Presbyterian Church since childhood. "Have you experienced inviting Jesus Christ to come into your heart — to forgive your sins and save your soul?" I asked. "No," he muttered. Two hours later, he died — unsaved!

Salvation is an urgent need. Death would come without a schedule. Dennis J. DeHaan's "Perhaps Today!" admonition concerning Christ's Second Coming may also relate to the possibility of our own death. Perhaps today, who knows? Death comes like a thief in the night. What is 70 years of life on earth and a billion years in hell? We need salvation from God's wrath because of our sins and imperfections. Faith in Christ's substitutionary death solves this sin-problem we have with God. All we need is to COME, BELIEVE, RELY ON or TRUST in Him. How can we pay no attention to our eternal life and future? "[H]ow will we escape if we neglect so great a salvation?" (Heb. 2:3a)

Yes, salvation is an urgent need! Too much hesitation hinders a man from having the born-again experience. Life on earth is glorious, but our eternal life in heaven with Christ and the angels of God surpasses a thousand earthly lives. Let's be with Christ forever by faith. It would be a life with the Creator and Owner of the Universe, our Lord Jesus. Our earthly goals are nothing compared with Christ's promised eternal home in heaven with the Holy Spirit and our Father God.

A Complete Dependence upon Christ Marks a Man's Born-Again Experience

When Adam and Eve disobeyed God, they heard their Maker calling: "Where are you?" From that time on God continued to call on the fallen man through His divine love and concern, sometimes in the form of afflictions or calamities.

There are so many instances in life where we seem to have been bitten by the "fiery serpents" of extreme affliction and distress. And this is where we come to realize our absolute need for Someone Bigger.

Have you seen a tough man among wrestlers? Watch him fall as dead. Then, as if by the stroke of pure mental discipline and determination, he would "resurrect" to life again in full strength. One wrestler stood still as if telling the man before him, "you can never beat me by your own poor strength!" Without responding, he allowed his opponent to box and kick him for a time; but he could not be moved. Disgusted, his opponent started biting his scalp and then pounding the wound until blood oozed down his cheeks. But the tough guy just stayed on.

Think of the insanity of wrestling. That's how madly tough man is against the clarion call of the Lord in the form of pains and trials. Man won't humble down before the Lord, as with dying Voltaire who said: "the love of God does not mention that man [Christ]."

Therefore, "Blessed are the poor in spirit (or those who don't have the fighting spirit!), for theirs is the kingdom of heaven." Blessed are those who considered themselves helpless against the venomous sting of sin, for they'll completely trust in the Savior Jesus. Spurgeon said that the door of heaven is too low, that it is impossible to enter without stooping. Genuine humility, we may add, is best shown by that giraffe of old who bent his long neck and knees just to enter the door of Noah's ark.

Charles Finney was a great revivalist. He was an aspiring lawyer then, before his conversion. God's grace, however, dawned upon him when he started asking himself, "Charles, what will you do after passing the bar?" He imagined himself becoming much fulfilled in the practice of law until he reached the point where he asked himself: "After retiring, what will I do?" The idea of death exploded into his mind until that small, still voice of conscience jammed into his subconscious with the words, "You'll be judged, Charles, you'll be judged!"

It was that very moment in his life when Finney was being bitten by the poisonous snake of conviction; and where he looked at Christ for help.

The born-again experience, therefore, is complete dependence upon Christ for everything since He is the Lord of life and the only Redeemer of man.

Double-Mindedness Bars a Man from Having a Born-Again Experience

One wicked old man told his friends it was still too early to think about religion until his doctor told him he was dying. As if beating a very pressing deadline, he went around the neighborhood looking for a priest, a pastor, or a Mormon elder—anyone who looks like a saint! One thing was burning in his mind, though: he was dying and unsaved—his conscience told him he was guilty before God!

The Bible says that today is the day of salvation (Cf. 2 Cor. 6:2). God knows that if you won't accept Christ today as Lord and Savior of your soul, then you'll do the same to Him tomorrow—reject Him in your heart as much as you can! Paul said that as a man gets older, so he will "proceed from bad to worse, deceiving and being deceived." Man is one step more wicked daily in the heart; he is one step away from heaven—yes, one step gospel-hardened every tick of the clock!

Wrote Billy Graham that all are improving except man. For he is spiritually dead, incapable of absorbing the things of God. Newspaper reports tell us that some habitual criminals are diploma-holders, graduates from great universities. Hitler, Marcos, among other dictators, were known as bookworms. Cuba's dictator Fidel Castro was a former Jesuit priest. Great schools may produce outstanding scholars. But only Christ can give the man a new heart—can produce saints out of demoniacs; or the Magdalenes, the thieves, the Sauls, the Zacchaeuses of this world. Yes, in Christ, man can be born again!

But too much doubt bars a man from having a born-again experience.

Many choose to laugh at the doctrine of the second birth as if God's own plan for man's entrance to His kingdom—that is the necessity to be reborn! — is worthy of man's evil sarcasm. They have seen truly born-again men and women. But their hearts are simply too wicked to believe in Christ and His words.

The hour will come, however, when their little brains will become much brighter; their memory, stronger; their conscience, sharper to notice the need of the second birth. And that very hour will be at the day of reckoning when their guilt will send them trembling in fear before the sole Judge of heaven and earth, Christ Jesus (Cf. Acts 10:42). Not only that, for God will cause them to remember that one day they were being warned through reading this little piece of work.

A Genuine Biblical Faith Ushers a Man's Born-Again Experience

Do you want the second birth or the born-again experience as demanded by Christ? We ask this question because God cannot work with your regeneration outside of your will to believe, trust, and rely upon Jesus. We underscored elsewhere in this material that Christ Himself enlightens every man. (John 1:9) That is why Christ did not perform many miracles in Nazareth because of the people's unbelief despite His illuminative and hallowed presence. (Matt. 13:57-58) Every person got enlightened because of Christ's resurrection and omnipresence, as when two or three gathered in His name. Unbelief, thus, is irrational. The doctrine is that, given our Christ-caused enlightenment, we must seek God and His salvation in our hearts through Jesus, the Only Way to the Father. We haven't read from the Scriptures of Christ's answering the needs of those who don't need Him. Bartimaeus, Zacchaeus, the bleeding woman, the paralytic man (lowered from the roof)—all sought Christ's audience before our Lord healed them. When Christ healed the sick man at Bethesda, He first asked him if he would "wish to get well?" (John 5:6) As with Lazarus, Martha and Mary approached Christ and expressed their belief in our Lord's power to resurrect their brother. All in all, Christ would recognize and give rebirth to all believers who would accept and trust His lordship and role as Savior, God the Son, and Forgiver of sins. Jesus did not reply to the request of the unbelieving thief on the cross because He wanted him to seek the kingdom of God. The thief's "Jesus, save Yourself" sarcasm didn't work. Predestination, therefore, is just not Christ's platform to save humanity from hell. The hyper-Calvinists erred miserably and dangerously in their 5-point Calvinism. We need to believe, and the act of seeking Jesus in our hearts is one element of faith that satisfies God. It is the character of the genuine biblical faith as when the bleeding woman (for twelve years) threw herself into the crowd just she could "touch the fringe of His cloak." (Matt. 9:20-22)

Your salvation wouldn't happen by saying, "Lord, if you choose me before the foundation of the world, save me now. Let's talk about my faith in You next time." Well, your election before the world began does not have a hint of the Calvinistic predestination. God does not save a soul by the force of His will, since it is not how God's love works. "It was for freedom that Christ set us free." (Gal. 5:1) Love survives only in the climate of freedom, not in coercion, even if we termed the latter beautifully as God's irresistible grace. Second, God cannot save a soul outside of Christ. "For this reason," wrote the apostle Paul, "I endure all things for the sake of those who are chosen, so that they also may obtain the salvation which is in Christ Jesus." (2 Tim. 2:10) Yes, Paul endured sufferings just to help the elect "obtain the salvation which is in Christ Jesus."

The Spirit of God is urging you to bend the knees of your heart at this moment that you may acknowledge and confess your sinfulness and lack of love for Christ Jesus in your old Christless life. Be humble before our Unseen God, and by faith, receive Christ into your heart as your only Lord and personal Savior. Do it now! And you will live forever, says the Lord. For he "who believes in the Son has eternal life." (John 3:36a)

We don't need to memorize all the teachings from the Bible to receive forgiveness and salvation from Christ. "Trust in the

Lord with all your heart And do not lean on your own understanding." (Prov. 3:5) For "faith is the assurance of things hoped for, the conviction of things not seen." (Heb. 11:1)

Christ told Nicodemus that "whoever believes may in Him have eternal life." From this Scripture (in John 3:14), we find in just eight words the key to the second birth. No misinterpretation can break into this 8-word truth: "WHOEVER BELIEVES MAY IN HIM HAVE ETERNAL LIFE." So clear that faith in Jesus precedes the born again event.

As penned by Habakkuk:

"Behold, as for the proud one,
His soul is not right within him;
But the RIGHTEOUS will LIVE by his FAITH." (Hab. 2:4)

The nutshell of the born-again experience is faith in Jesus Christ—the biblical formula to LIVE FOREVER!

Live forever, my friend. Wrote the apostle Paul: "Behold, now is 'the acceptable time,' behold, now is 'the day of salvation.' (2 Cor. 6:2) This moment is your hour of salvation. Tomorrow may never come.

Believe in Jesus Christ and receive Him in your heart as your only Lord and Savior. If you don't, be patient. Review some chapters. If you do, we've concluded this work. God bless your newfound faith in Jesus! God bless your soul for the sake of Christ. Amen.

ABOUT THE AUTHOR

Jun P. Espina loves nature, music, painting, and poetry but couldn't find inner joy during his first 27 years of life. After his father's death, he taught in college and met religious friends who couldn't satisfy his search for meaning. In 1984, he got converted to the biblical Christian faith. He married his girlfriend, Virgie, the following year—God blessed them with three children—and served Christ as a believer in different spaces of the Christian ministry. After over 30 years of orthodox Christianity, he wrote few Christian eBooks in his home in Davao City. Sometimes his four little grandchildren played with their smartphones by his side.

OTHER BOOK BY THE AUTHOR

PENTECOSTALISM, ITS THEOLOGY & THE CHARISMATIC CHAOS REVISITED: Reexamining the Scriptural Works of the Holy Spirit on Miracles, Speaking in Tongues, and Church Worship of Extreme Pentecostalism